Jossey-Bass Teacher

Jossey-Bass Teacher provides K–12 teachers with essential knowledge and tools to create a positive and life-long impact on student learning. Trusted and experienced educational mentors offer practical classroom-tested and theory-based teaching resources for improving teaching practice in a broad range of grade levels and subject areas. From one educator to another, we want to be your first source to make every day your best day in teaching. *Jossey-Bass Teacher* resources serve two types of informational needs—essential knowledge and essential tools.

Essential knowledge resources provide the foundation, strategies, and methods from which teachers may design curriculum and instruction to challenge and excite their students. Connecting theory to practice, essential knowledge books rely on a solid research base and time-tested methods, offering the best ideas and guidance from many of the most experienced and well-respected experts in the field.

Essential tools save teachers time and effort by offering proven, ready-to-use materials for in-class use. Our publications include activities, assessments, exercises, instruments, games, ready reference, and more. They enhance an entire course of study, a weekly lesson, or a daily plan. These essential tools provide insightful, practical, and comprehensive materials on topics that matter most to K–12 teachers.

The Heart of Teaching

The Heart of Teaching

Creating High-Impact Lessons for the Adolescent Learner

Audrey J. Sirota
with contributions by
Laura Ianacone Taschek

Foreword by Roland Tharp

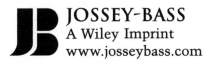
JOSSEY-BASS
A Wiley Imprint
www.josseybass.com

Published by Jossey-Bass
A Wiley Imprint
989 Market Street, San Francisco, CA 94103-1741   www.josseybass.com

Limit of Liability/Disclaimer of Warranty: While the publisher and author have used their best efforts in preparing this book, they make no representations or warranties with respect to the accuracy or completeness of the contents of this book and specifically disclaim any implied warranties of merchantability or fitness for a particular purpose. No warranty may be created or extended by sales representatives or written sales materials. The advice and strategies contained herein may not be suitable for your situation. You should consult with a professional where appropriate. Neither the publisher nor author shall be liable for any loss of profit or any other commercial damages, including but not limited to special, incidental, consequential, or other damages.

Readers should be aware that Internet Web sites offered as citations and/or sources for further information may have changed or disappeared between the time this was written and when it is read.

Jossey-Bass books and products are available through most bookstores. To contact Jossey-Bass directly call our Customer Care Department within the U.S. at 800-956-7739, outside the U.S. at 317-572-3986, or fax 317-572-4002.

Jossey-Bass also publishes its books in a variety of electronic formats. Some content that appears in print may not be available in electronic books.

Library of Congress Cataloging-in-Publication Data

Sirota, Audrey J., date.
  The heart of teaching : creating high-impact lessons for the adolescent learner / Audrey J. Sirota, with contributions by Laura Ianacone Taschek ; foreword by Roland Tharp. — 1st ed.
      p. cm.
  Includes bibliographical references and index.
ISBN-13 978-0-7879-7802-0 (alk. paper)
ISBN-10 0-7879-7802-7 (alk. paper)
  1. High school teaching. 2. Effective teaching. 3. Motivation in education. 4. Teacher-student relationships. I. Taschek, Laura Ianacone. II. Title.
LB1737.A3S57 2006
  373.1102—dc22   2005023381

Printed in the United States of America
FIRST EDITION
PB Printing   10 9 8 7 6 5 4 3 2 1

Contents

List of Tables, Figures, Exhibits, and Handouts   ix

Foreword by Roland Tharp   xi

Preface   xiii

Acknowledgments   xvii

The Authors   xix

Introduction: Creating a Meaningful Classroom Environment   1
Opportunities and Challenges   2
Solutions   4
Conclusion   7

1.   Teachers and Students Producing Together: Joint Productive Activity—Collaboration or Bust!   9
Research Support for Joint Productive Activities   10
Working with Adolescents   11
Creating Lessons with Joint Activities   12
Assessment of Joint Activities   13
Introduction to Laura Ianacone Taschek   13
Lessons from the Classroom   15
Lesson 1: Literature, Grade 10   15
Lesson 2: Biology, Grade 9   17
Lesson 3: World History, Grade 10   22
Conclusion   29

2.   Developing Language and Literacy Across the Curriculum   31
Scaffolding Instruction   32
Lessons from the Classroom   33
Lesson 1: Geometry, Grade 9 or 10   33
Lesson 2: Earth Sciences, Grade 10 or 11   36
Lesson 3: Sheltered English, Grades 9 to 12   40
Lesson 4: Global Studies, Grades 11 and 12   44
Conclusion   52

3. Contextualization or Making Meaning: Connecting School to Students' Lives 53

    Contextualizing Instruction Within the Community 54
    Contextualizing Lessons and Activities 56
    Lessons from the Classroom 57
    Lesson 1: Language Arts/History, Grade 8 58
    Lesson 2: Biology, Grade 9 or 10 61
    Lesson 3: World History/Geography, Grades 9 and 10 65
    Lesson 4: History/Social Studies, Grade 9 or 10 69
    Conclusion 72

4. Challenging Activities: Teaching Complex Thinking 75

    Lessons from the Classroom 76
    Lesson 1: Literature, Grade 9 or 10 77
    Lesson 2: Social Science, Grades 9 to 11 84
    Lesson 3: Trigonometry, Grade 11 87
    Lesson 4: Writing Research Papers, Grades 9 to 12 90
    Conclusion 95

5. Teaching Through Dialogue: The Instructional Conversation 97

    The Teacher's Role 98
    Planning Lessons with Instructional Conversations 99
    Benefits of the Instructional Conversation 99
    Structuring the Instructional Conversation 100
    Organizing Conversational Activities 100
    Lessons from the Classroom 105
    Lesson 1: Biology, Grades 10 and 11 105
    Lesson 2: Global Studies, Grades 10 to 12 113
    Conclusion 120

    Conclusion: A Model of Assistance 123

Appendix 1: Creating and Managing Classroom Learning Centers 127

    Organizing the Centers 128
    Classroom Groupings 129
    Group Management and Discipline 129
    Scheduling Center Activities 131
    Learning Center Assessment 131
    Conclusion 132

Appendix 2: Laurellos Castle 133

Appendix 3: Tibet Questions Graphic Organizer 137

Notes 139

Index 145

List of Tables, Figures, Exhibits, and Handouts

Tables

4.1   Research Paper Rubric   93
5.1   Schedule for Classroom Conversation   103
5.2   Global Issues Lesson Design   114
A-1.1   Learning Center Rights and Responsibilities   130

Figures

I.1   Diversification of Activities   6
3.1   Culture Wheel Template   67
3.2   Student's Culture Wheel   67
3.3   Universal Culture Wheel   69
A.2   Laurellos Castle   133
A.3   Tibet Questions Graphic Organizer   137

Exhibits

1.1   Assessment Rubric for the Castle Activity   28
2.1   Rubric for Tent Construction Activity   35
2.2   Sample of Student Work for Expository Reading   43
2.3   Rubric for Grading Literary Responses: Environment Unit   50
3.1   Examples of Student Quick-Writes   59
3.2   Collage Project Rubric   63
4.1   Maya Angelou Literary Analysis Rubric   80
4.2   Maya Angelou Editorial Writing Assignment Rubric   82
5.1   Instructional Conversation Sequence   101
5.2   Participation Structure Cards   104
5.3   Samples of Student Work on the War and Conflict Unit   121
A-1.1   Middle Ages Grade and Criteria Sheet   132

Handouts

1.1   Create an Island: Student Instructions   19
1.2   Create an Island: Reflection Questions   21
1.3   Castle Questions   24
1.4   Castle-Building Activity   25
2.1   Plate Tectonics Word Web Activity   38
2.2   What's a Word Web?   39
2.3   The Properties of Food   42
2.4   Quick-Write Activity   48
2.5   Research Tasks for PowerPoint Presentation   49
3.1   Instructions for the Collage Project   62
3.2   Families of the Coastside   71
4.1   Student Assignment for *I Know Why the Caged Bird Sings*   81
4.2   Student Assignment for "Our Environment: Global Warming"   86
5.1   Student Assignment for the Global Reading Center
       Human Rights Task: What Is a War Crime?   116

Foreword

Teaching is a noble profession. We use *noble* because teaching is underpaid, under-acknowledged, supremely important, and infinitely challenging. And *noble* also because its practice allows, even demands, the involvement of the teacher's every capacity: knowledge, discipline, craft, energy, spirit, and heart. Teaching is both mind and heart, and to achieve its nobility, it must be practiced with both. The teaching approach made visible in this book offers not only inspiration but practical guides to action.

In previous centuries, a simplistic psychology assumed that teachers pour knowledge from mind to mind, from teacher's mind to student's, with pitchers of lectures, assignments, and diagrams. It was assumed that good teachers could be measured by the depth of their subject matter knowledge, by the contents of their own minds. The acts of teaching were largely ignored; after all, pouring is pouring, and what matters is what is poured. And it is up to the student to get it.

Psychological science now knows that is not true. As you will read in this book, there is also a heart of teaching, as well as a mind. That heart consists of the interactions between teacher and students and of the organization of instructional activities. Those elements are what we call *pedagogy*. The practice of this psychologically valid pedagogy enables teachers to program for each student the assistance each requires. As you will read, this is not a visionary dream but a practical, achievable standard.

Pedagogy is sometimes thought to be the domain of primary and elementary teaching, whereas content expertise is the domain of secondary teachers, as if there were a divide between heart and mind somewhere in middle school. So it appears, on the surface: trigonometry is more complex than learning to count. But recent research gives a more complex view: *neither pedagogy nor content knowledge alone is sufficient for effective teaching and learning*—not for students of any developmental level or age. We know now that the solution lies in content pedagogy, which expresses subject matter in valid processes of human interaction and activity.

In *The Heart of Teaching,* Audrey Sirota and Laura Ianacone Taschek appear to concentrate on pedagogy, and well they should, because it has had so little emphasis in high school teaching. But a more subtle reading of this book will reveal throughout a goal of content pedagogy in which the heart of teaching is joined with its mind. Few realize that effective pedagogy can make a big difference in motivating students and enhancing their learning.

Audrey Sirota knows this well. I was privileged to work with her for a decade in the Center for Research on Education, Diversity and Excellence (CREDE). Our research there established reliable pedagogies for students of diverse cultures, races, languages, and incomes. As a principal figure in CREDE's study and practice of professional development for teachers, she lived and worked in schools, bringing our science to classrooms and helping teachers to practice their noble profession in ways that foster student achievement and, by bringing the heart into teaching, restore its joy.

Roland Tharp
Research Professor
University of California, Berkeley

Preface

During a recent teachers' conference, several colleagues and I began to discuss the reasons we entered the field of teaching. A couple of them, dissatisfied with their jobs, had come to the field as part of a career change. Another recounted that she did not know what else to do. Her close friend told the story of how he was groomed to take over his father's commercial business. However, a very short time into his business career, his father, sensing his dissatisfaction, encouraged him to pursue his dream of coaching high school basketball. Three of us recounted that we knew we wanted to be teachers from a very young age. My first teaching experience began when I was eight years old—the year I began a summer camp for "little kids."

What I learned that summer and in the successive summers of running the camp have been critical to my teaching: build a strong community that is inclusive of everyone's needs; speak to students in ways that they can relate to and understand; listen carefully to what they have to say because they will tell me what they know and what they are struggling with; allow and support my students to express themselves in meaningful ways, whether through writing and poetry, music and singing, painting, theater, solving mathematical equations, playing soccer, or conducting science experiments; and strive always to be learning along with my students.

Fourteen years later, I found myself in front of my first classroom. The lessons I learned back then carried me through my first teaching experiences. After learning effective classroom management techniques and getting trained in conflict resolution, it was possible to build inclusive communities and offer exciting curriculum, instruction, and assessments. Over the next two decades, after teaching kindergarten through university students and studying sociocultural theory and its applications to classroom teaching and learning, I realized that the heart of teaching rests in introspection and reflection.

This book is a series of practical stories about how many teachers have worked together to modify their thinking and, consequently, their instructional lessons to make them more meaningful and relevant to students' lives. The book contains examples from the disciplines of language arts, mathematics, sciences, and social sciences. Many of the lessons were developed and revised from a collaborative effort between several teachers and me. In these cases, I have used a single fictional name to highlight the teachers who collaborated. Other lessons were mainly created by one teacher. I have indicated that teacher with her/his first and last names.

Laura Ianacone Taschek, my colleague and an exemplary high school social science teacher, has made special contributions to the creation of this book. She had the courage to be vulnerable, revealing her frustrations as well as dreams. "How do I make my lessons more meaningful for my students? How do I get them to care?" From her inquiries emerged a collaboration. Laura and I began working together and with other teachers to create lessons that are engaging and challenging to students. We want students' voices to be represented in the class through dialogue and their writing as well as collaborative presentations.

The Heart of Teaching is intended to be used as a practical guide for teachers. It poses reflective questions that we can use to consider the material we teach and the manner in which we teach. The framework and principles in the book can be used to strengthen routine lessons, making them meaningful and appropriately challenging to students. In addition, the principles are applicable and can help motivate all students, especially English Language Learners and other students who are placed at risk due to social, cultural, racial, ethnic, economic, or geographical factors.

The principles delineated in the book have been researched and documented by the Center for Research on Education, Diversity and Excellence (CREDE). Here, they are applied to the work of high school teaching and learning. The principles serve as the template for this book. The ideas were introduced by Lev Vygotsky in his description of human development and later developed for classroom teaching and learning. The principles document how people learn best: through collaborative, meaningful, and challenging activities that require participation through talking, writing, and thinking about relevant ideas. These principles were developed and served as the framework for the Kamehameha Early Education Project, the National Center for Research on Cultural Diversity and Second Language, and, most recently, CREDE. The work of CREDE has been extensive, spanning over eight years and sponsoring the work of over thirty national and international research projects. CREDE's mission was to move the educational issues of diversity and excellence to the forefront of educational discussions and research. Through my work with CREDE, I had the opportunity to work with this large and thoughtful group of middle and high school teachers.

Each of the five chapters in *The Heart of Teaching* demonstrates an application and a rationale for one of the principles. It then presents a set of focus questions that helps teachers design and reflect on their instructional lessons. As you read each chapter, you will walk through a series of lesson plans that tell stories of how high school teachers took these principles and made them meaningful to their teaching practice. In most examples, the full lesson is presented, including an assessment component. Following the lesson, the teacher uses the focus questions to analyze and reflect on her or his teaching and make changes to the lesson to increase its relevance, meaning, and applicability. Laura Ianacone Taschek took the ideas and transformed her teaching to incorporate the principles into her social studies classes. Each chapter contains a section that highlights her work with her students.

The Introduction lays out the rationale and theoretical foundation for the book and briefly reviews the salient issues in American public education. It proposes a redefinition of the teacher's role as a facilitator and coach of learning who invests in asking reflective, analytical questions about what and how we are teaching.

Chapter One defines the principle of joint or collaborative activity. It provides a strong rationale for doing collaborative work with adolescent learners and expounds on the teacher's role as well as issues of assessment. Chapter Two focuses on the principle of language development, which serves as the foundation of all teaching and learning. The chapter proposes that all teachers, whether they are instructing in the language of history, biology, or trigonometry, are actually language teachers. In addition to presenting several core content lessons, it includes a lesson for English Language Development instruction. Chapter Three introduces the principle of contextualized instruction, defined as making school meaningful and relevant to students' lives. It explores the issues of the diversity of our student populations; cultural compatibility of the curriculum, instruction, and assessments; and schema development. Chapter Four addresses the principle of cognitively complex thinking. Most of the lessons contain two versions: an initial version and an improved version where the teacher has reflected on the changes that need to be made in order to increase the complexity and relevance of the activity. In this chapter, teachers involve students in the assessment process so that they understand the expectations (as laid out in a rubric form) and have a gauge to evaluate their own performance. Finally, in Chapter Five, the principles merge into a single teaching method as the instructional conversation is presented. The instructional conversation provides a forum in which students and the teacher can talk about their ideas in a meaningful context. The conversation is goal driven, cognitively challenging, and collaboratively constructed. It demands student participation and requires them to use the academic language of instruction. The Conclusion leaves us to consider the humanity of public schools for both students and teachers. In order to do our job well, we need support and assistance just as our students need our support, whether that is by creating teacher teams or collaborative study groups. By tapping into each other's expertise and resources, we find a wealth of knowledge, insight, thoughtfulness, and commitment.

Acknowledgments

As we walk through our lives, we are all touched by many people and occurrences that set the stage for our future endeavors. This book was created by such a set of circumstances. *The Heart of Teaching* is truly a tribute to the magic that can happen when we work collaboratively.

I thank my primary collaborator, Laura Ianacone Taschek. She had the vision and energy to apply these principles to her high school classroom. She became an exemplary model for both new and veteran teachers who took her systems and structures and applied them to their own classrooms. I thank all the teachers who followed Laura's lead and took the risk to work collaboratively, creating meaningful and motivating activities for their students. Many thanks to the teaching assistants of 1999 who dedicated themselves to the development of these principles: Maria Cavanaugh-Reitano, Marina Escobar-Greatorex, Sara Goldfarb, Pilar Gray-Luzzi, Gina Guardino, Ann Haines, Shawna Hodovance, Diane Ichikawa, Mara Mills, Molly O'Neil, Socorro Reyes, Tina Schwab, and Caitlin Spohrer. Special thanks to Jack Mallory for his flexibility, openness, and creativity. He allowed Laura the room to experiment and then went on to create a series of thoughtful learning centers to help his students connect to the realities and heartache of war. Also many thanks to Santa Cruz High School for opening its doors to innovative thinking and projects.

Many thanks to the hundreds of students who have been my teachers, guiding me every step of the way with their praise as well as constructive criticism. And many thanks to the dozens of teachers who have also been my teachers. You truly are an open-minded, flexible, creative, thoughtful, committed, brilliant group of people.

This book would not have been possible without the vision and work of Roland Tharp and Ronald Gallimore, who first outlined these principles formally in *Rousing Minds to Life*. In 1995, I remember vividly sitting in a graduate course and meeting Tharp for the first time. He stepped onto a small, narrow stage and began to speak about the principles outlined in this book. After a few moments, it was as if the walls disappeared, the stage enlarged, and the ideas I had been putting into practice for over a decade were declared, validated, and given a language. I wanted all teachers to have access to these principles, for they validate the effective teaching and learning that many of us are manifesting in our classrooms.

Through my association with Tharp and Barry Rutherford at the Center for Research on Education, Diversity and Excellence, I have had the opportunity to teach these principles to many teachers over the last few years. I acknowledge and thank the dozens of teachers who strive to apply these principles to their teaching. I express my gratitude to my first collaborators in experimenting with these principles in a professional development context: thanks to Stephanie Dalton, Peggy Estrada, Susan Freeman, and all the students/teachers who took Education 250.

I gratefully thank my first mentor in teaching and learning who was practicing these principles before we had names for them: Gloria Rainer. I also thank Irene McGinty and Noni Reis, who have been my mentors at Starlight Professional Development School. They share the ambition to practice these principles in both the classroom and in a professional development capacity. Thanks to Phyllis Gold, who is an authentic conflict resolution guru. She taught me how to differentiate between our needs and those of our students. Thanks to Cindy Meier, whose work, vision, and talent touch all of us who have the opportunity to work with her. And, finally, to Grace Mona Levin, who understood the importance of collaborative play.

I owe a debt of gratitude to my editor, Christie Hakim, for her clarity, vision, flexibility, and ability to hold my hand when needed. Also, many thanks to Beverly Miller and Sarah Rabkin for their feedback and editorial expertise. Thanks to Sarah and Christie for holding an unwavering faith that I had something important to share. A basket of thanks to my dear friend Andrea, who encouraged me and initially helped me get the manuscript in a presentable and readable form. If there has been an oversight and I have failed to thank someone who contributed to this body of work, this is in no way intentional. Please accept my appreciation for your valued contribution.

And, of course, this book would never have been possible without the support and love of my parents, grandparents, family, and friends. Thanks for cheering the work on and on and on, providing the most incredible child care and standing by the work all these years: Jeffrey, Karen, and Genevieve; Howard and Connie; Aunt Charlotte and the Chicago clan; Aunt Hazel and the Arizona clan; Nate and Ken; Rachel and Julie; Maryasha and Hannah; Kendell, Cheri, and Mirannda; Christina; Sigrid Ann; Drea; Deb; the true poet and writer of my family, Alison Apotheker, who has always held an unwavering belief in my teaching; and Elsa, who taught me about the deeper meanings of inclusion. Thanks to Mom for encouraging and supporting me to expand and explore in both life and my teaching career. And a huge thank-you to Hannah and Fiona for being my loving collaborators in life.

The Authors

Audrey Sirota has spent the majority of her life in classroom settings. From her initial childhood experiences running a summer camp program to teaching preschoolers through university students over the past two decades, she is committed to providing quality educational experiences for her students, advancing the practice of teaching, and promoting an equitable education for all students.

Sirota currently operates her own educational business, which includes professional development consulting for local school districts, facilitating and leading workshops for teachers, professional writing, and running a preschool. Her school district consulting involves working closely with teachers to facilitate collaborative teacher meetings, study groups, and action research projects. She focuses on examining curriculum, instructional methods, and assessment practices. She has also been on the faculty of the University of California, where she taught courses in literacy development and educational theory. In addition, she worked with the Center for Research on Education, Diversity and Excellence (CREDE) for several years. CREDE is a research-based center that focuses on students placed at risk of educational failure due to linguistic, racial, economic, or geographic factors. While there, she served as professional development specialist supporting student teachers as well as new and veteran elementary and high school teachers to examine their teaching practice.

Being both an artist and an educator, Sirota has also worked for Tucson's Pima County Adult Education's Project R.A.I.S.E., teaching literacy and the arts to developmentally challenged adults, danced professionally with the Barbara Mettler Dance Company, and served as the educational director for a women's theater company in Tucson, Arizona.

She received her bachelor's degree and teaching credential from the University of Illinois and master's degree from the University of California.

Laura Ianacone Taschek, a daughter, granddaughter, and niece of teachers, teaches social studies at Lake Braddock Secondary School in Fairfax County, Virginia, where she also serves as a mentor teacher. Before beginning her graduate studies, she worked at the National Clearing House for Bilingual Education. She received her master's degree in secondary education from the University of California at Santa Cruz in 1998, also serving as a teaching assistant for Audrey Sirota and others, and began her teaching career at Half Moon Bay High School in the Cabrillo Unified School District in Half Moon Bay, California.

The Heart of Teaching

Introduction: Creating a Meaningful Classroom Environment

A good school for anyone is a little like kindergarten and a little like a good post-graduate program—the two ends of the educational spectrum, at which we understand that we cannot treat any two human beings identically, but must take into account their special interests and styles even as we hold all to high and rigorous standards.

Deborah Meier, *The Power of Their Ideas* **(1995)**

I have been teaching for nineteen years. Like all other teachers, I take pride in the years I have put into my teaching career and in the hundreds of students who have walked through my classroom doors. Like my peers, I look back on a career rich with success stories, as well as stories of challenge and heartache.

Over the course of this career, my students have pushed me to think about questions that I might otherwise not have considered—essential questions such as, "Why are we studying this stuff? What difference will this make in my life? In one year, in five years, am I going to remember any of this anyway?"

More thought-provoking questions also emerged: "What is meaningful about life? What makes us happy? What saddens us? What works about our life? What is challenging? How can we make our lives more meaningful? If we could do anything in life, what would it be?"

There was an onslaught of questions, and then my own began: "How can I make this curriculum meaningful to my students' lives? How can I address their needs and desires with this pre-scripted, state-mandated curriculum? How can I capture the interest and enthusiasm that I see during passing time and lunch time as they talk to their friends? What do they need right now and how can I best serve their needs?"

And I began to consider even weightier questions: "Why are some of my students succeeding within this system and others failing? Who succeeds and who fails year after year? Why do the high school dropout rates mirror the prison rates for young African American and Hispanic men? What can schools do to support students to succeed within the academic system? What can schools do to meet the needs of English Language Learners? What can teachers do? What can I do?"

Emerging from these questions came the beginnings of a reconceptualization of my teaching: what I was doing in my classroom, how I was doing it, and why.

Opportunities and Challenges

Changing demographics, reform teaching methods, and philosophical theories all present teachers with opportunities to integrate new ideas and ways of thinking into their teaching practice. Often these opportunities also present challenges to our way of thinking and teaching.

Changing Demographics

Over the past several decades, the population of children attending American public schools has changed significantly. The classroom community now includes larger numbers of students from diverse cultures and ethnicities, children of single-parent families, and children who live in poverty.[1] According to the Census Bureau statistics from 2001, one-fifth of America's school-age children speak a language other than English in their home. In half of these households, the dominant language is Spanish.[2] "Between 1990 and 2000, the population of K–12 students learning English as a second language in U.S. public schools doubled from 2.2 million to 4.4. million," according to the Office of English Language Acquisition in the U.S. Department of Education.[3] How does this linguistic and cultural diversity affect our work as educators? What opportunities and what challenges does it present?

The Teaching Force

During the past century, two generations of adults have grown up in a period of atypically low immigration. Since many teachers received training at the time when immigration was at a low point, teacher education programs did not address the cultural and linguistic diversity of today's student population. In addition, many teachers attended public school in the 1950s and 1960s, before desegregation. Consequently, many attended homogeneous neighborhood schools.[4] Therefore, many of today's teachers have little personal knowledge and experience growing up in classrooms with racial, cultural, and linguistic diversity. How can we become effective teachers for the current student population given our own backgrounds and experiences? What can we do in our classrooms to offer quality curricula, effective instructional strategies, and meaningful assessments to a diverse student body?

Who Does Well? The Paradigm of Public Education

Every autumn, year after year, we see similar statistics on the students who score well and those who score poorly on standardized tests. Over the past two decades, statistical data consistently reveal that white, middle-class, European American males tend to score the highest on standardized tests. Women and students from culturally diverse communities score substantially lower on these same tests.[5]

These statistics are no surprise to many educators. We frequently discuss how the public school system was designed and still functions with European, middle-class values. These statistics explain why, as of October 2000, of the people living in the United States between the ages of eighteen and twenty-four with less than a high school education, 27.8 percent were Hispanics, 13.1 percent were blacks, and 6.9 percent were whites.[6] The students who are doing poorly on standardized test scores are often the same ones who are dropping out of the school system.

Along with race, economics also plays a pivotal role in determining who succeeds and who fails in school. The National Center for Educational Statistics reveals that "in 2000, young adults living in families with incomes in the lowest 20 percent of our nation were six times as likely as their peers to drop out of high school."[7]

Lack of Relevance

There are many plausible explanations for why school is not working for many teens. Economic and social pressures present real concerns for many young people, distracting them from schoolwork. Unfortunately, much of what we teach in our schools is unrelated or, at best, distantly related to what is happening in students' lives. The gap between salient issues students face on a daily basis and the state-mandated core curriculum can be wide. Once school curricula and instruction lose their relevance and meaning, students' motivation tends to drop. Life's demands take the forefront, leaving little, if any, room for satisfaction in school.

How can we create a bridge between these two worlds? We know that we profoundly influence the lives of our students. How can we use the school curricula as a vehicle for helping students explore meaningful topics and construct thoughtful solutions to pressing concerns? How can the school curricula help students solve problems with intelligence and compassion?

History Tells Us . . .

Questions like the ones I have posed above are not new to American education reformers. Experts in multicultural curriculum and equity pedagogy have long lamented the lack of relevance in school curricula—relevance to the real concerns of students' lives and to society's problems.[8] They point to inappropriately homogenized, regimented school curricula that ignore and suppress students' backgrounds, individuality, and different learning styles. Standard curricula and instruction are designed not to teach students to think critically, say critics, but rather to create an obedient labor force. Poor, minority, and working-class students are tracked into blue-collar positions, while middle- and upper-class students are tracked into managerial and professional jobs.[9] The status quo is purposefully maintained. Certain curricula are withheld from students who do not attend higher-level or Advanced Placement courses.

In addition, access to academic language and content is limited in lower-level classes. Consequently, students are prevented from taking advantage of educational opportunities such as internships and college.

Over the past century, educational reformers have posited solutions such as the integration of democratic ideals in the classroom, the creation of "open" and "free" schools, the reorganization of school structures, the application of "reform" curricula and assessments, and the movement from teacher-centered to student-centered classrooms.

In the Reagan era, with the *Nation at Risk* report, we saw a strong push for a back-to-basics curriculum.[10] Now we are witnessing a similar phenomenon with the No Child Left Behind Act. We are being squeezed to be accountable for our students' success as evidenced by standardized test scores. Both students and teachers are being held accountable.

Solutions

Finding solutions to the myriad of problems of public school education is an ongoing endeavor. It involves transforming our thinking about how schools function and the roles that students and teachers play.

How About Another Revolution?

It is only through a revolution—a radical transformation of the ways in which we think about both the students' roles and our roles in the classroom—that the face of high school teaching and learning will change.

What do we know now that we have not known before? We know that we must not succumb to the isolation that we have experienced as classroom teachers. Too often, we are encouraged to close the classroom door after the students enter so that no one can see how we and the students are performing. We are afraid to ask for help because we believe it is an indication of weakness. At the same time, we know we must collaborate with others to build curricula. We must share materials and resources during budgetary limitations and continual cutbacks. We must talk to each other, discuss our students' progress, construct joint themes and lessons, and share our workload. We must give feedback to our administrators and legislators and define what we need for our own professional growth.

Finally, we must find a balancing point between the pendulum swings of federal- and state-mandated curricula. The back-to-basics curriculum was as inappropriate as the whole language movement. The whole language movement did not directly support the explicit teaching of the structure of our language: syntax, grammar, and spelling. The back-to-basics movement pushed the learning of basic skills at the expense of deep comprehension work: analysis, synthesis, and evaluation. We must combine the best of both worlds—deep comprehension work with lessons in academic English within specific content areas—so that students have choices about what they can do with their education.

We want our students to be inspired to go to school because they want to and not just because it is required. And we cannot discover the conditions that make this possible without also addressing the optimal conditions for teacher learning. How can we create a meaningful learning environment where both teachers and adolescents thrive rather than simply survive? Teachers and students face enormous challenges within the educational system: overcrowded classrooms, lack of supplies and textbooks, limited school and classroom budgets, imposed state standards, top-down curricula, and mandatory standardized testing, among others. In the light of all these limitations, how can we create a safe and comfortable place where teachers and students can build a functional community? How can we create a community where we openly communicate with one another, share interests, debate ideas, and engage in academic exercises that speak to our own life experiences? How can we guide our students in this type of learning?

Modifying Our Teaching

Over the past two decades, I have had the opportunity to experiment with many ways of teaching. I have been the "sage on the stage," lecturing to my high school students on the human cell, nerve fibers, and hair follicles of the epidermis. For a time, I abdicated all lecturing in favor of hands-on experimentation with little, if any, teacher intervention—having been taught that the students would figure it out themselves if I did not interfere in their learning process.

Finally, I sought a balance between these two extremes. I learned that my role as a teacher required me to be an expert about the subject matter, a facilitator of learning activities, a coach in providing support and direction to my students, and a diagnostician in assessing my students' abilities and moving them to the next level of learning.

Part of my journey in teaching has included the opportunity to be a mentor teacher to both new and veteran teachers as well as an instructor of college courses in education. Consequently, all of the ideas provided here have been tried in both my own and many other teachers' classrooms. This book contains stories and reflections of how teachers and I worked together to examine what we have been doing in our classrooms. It provides examples of how to set up and maintain a positive, effective, and equitable classroom environment for both students and teachers. It offers an alternative lens through which we can examine our pedagogy. Finally, it provides a practical guide with concrete activities that we can use to diversify and improve our curriculum, instruction, and assessments.

Diversification

One of the biggest challenges for teachers is transforming lectures into hands-on learning activities. Many teachers are concerned that students will not gain access to the core subject matter material if they do not provide the information through direct instruction. Throughout the book, I advocate for the diversification of activities as exemplified in Figure I.1. If we lecture to students the majority of the time, there will not be time or space to apply these principles to our teaching.

I use this chart as a guide in structuring activities within my own classes. It provides a quick reference to evaluate the distribution of time and activities within my classes. And it reminds me of the importance of diversifying activities so that the learners have the opportunity to be engaged participants-collaborators in their own learning.

Background Theory

The concepts addressed in this book are derived from sociocultural theory. In the sociocultural model of teaching and learning, both teachers and students are integral to the process of learning. Unlike earlier educational theories that focused on students interacting with their environment, sociocultural theory highlights the importance of students interacting with their peers and the teacher. All learning occurs within a social and cultural context. Teaching is defined as assisted performance. This means that our

FIGURE I.1. DIVERSIFICATION OF ACTIVITIES

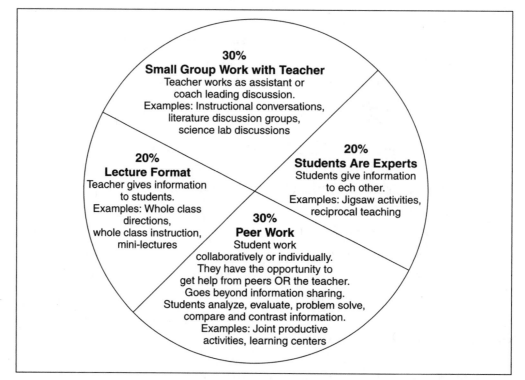

job as teachers is to help students move from one level of understanding and ability to the next, higher level. We are responsible for interacting with students in meaningful activities, assessing students' levels of understanding, and providing feedback and assistance to students about their work.

Out of this theory, Roland Tharp and his associates defined five pedagogy principles for teaching and learning:[11]

1. *Students and Teachers Producing Together:* Meaningful discussion accompanies collaboration between students and teachers.

2. *Developing Literacy and Language Across the Curriculum:* Teachers pay attention to when and how they develop students' academic language within specific content areas.

3. *Connecting School to Students' Lives:* The curriculum, instruction, and assessments take into account students' prior knowledge and experiences.

4. *Teaching Complex Thinking:* Instructional activities and assessments are appropriately challenging, meaningful, and stimulating. They push students to use higher-order thinking skills.

5. *Teaching Through Conversation:* Instruction is conversational and targets the students within their range of learning.

The most effective learning occurs when these principles of effective teaching and learning are put into practice. One of the most interesting attributes of these principles is that they transcend specific socioeconomic, cultural, racial, geographical, or language groups. Research demonstrates that the principles are effective with all students regardless of any risk factors. In fact, preliminary data reveal a positive relationship between teachers' use of these principles in their classes and student achievement on standardized tests.[12]

Conclusion

Reflecting on the changes that have taken place and continue to occur in education invites us to consider our place in history. What are we doing in our teaching, and how is it affecting our students' lives? Are we developing healthy, thoughtful people who can think deeply about our current issues? One hundred years from now, when our grandchildren read and listen to stories about the turn of the century, what legacy do we want to have left behind? The foundation of these principles is based on an understanding of human development. It offers a glimpse into how humans learn best. Does it not behoove us to apply this knowledge to our work in classrooms? To this end, we can help foster intelligent, thoughtful, compassionate human beings capable of dealing with the complex issues of our society.

Teachers and Students Producing Together
Joint Productive Activity—Collaboration or Bust!

Joint productive activities are experiences that require people to work together collaboratively, depending on each other and using each person's expertise. We are all socially and culturally accustomed to this type of interdependent learning; this our natural way of being human. Unfortunately, the frequency of joint productive activities declines as children progress through school, so that by high school, it is uncommon. Yet in the twenty-first century, this interdependence is a requirement for our global society. This chapter explains why collaborative learning approaches are important with adolescent students and how these can succeed in the classroom. Teaching using joint activities is fundamental to many of the lessons presented throughout this book.

Joint productive activities can help teachers diversify the learning that takes place in high school classrooms. These activities can be accomplished in pairs, small groups, or the whole class as a group. They can be as simple as asking students in pairs to discuss a question during a lecture, a strategy referred to as ***think pair share*** or ***pair share*** throughout the book.[1] During a recent lecture in a tenth-grade world history class, the teacher was discussing the effects of the industrial revolution in Europe, Japan, and the United States. After every ten minutes of the lecture, she would ask students to turn to their partner and discuss a prediction, summarization, or clarification question such as, "What impact do you think the industrial revolution had on schools—on how students were educated?" The product was simply students sharing their ideas with each other.

This same teacher also had her class participate in a whole-group joint activity by having each student write a part of a class book titled *The Effects of the Industrial Revolution on Europe, Japan, and the United States.* The entire class had to contribute a piece of the text to make it flow smoothly. They also had to work as a thirty-two-person team to create charts that compared and contrasted the effects on the different countries. Joint productive activities can occur within a short period of time, as evidenced in the pair share discussions. Conversely, they can take up large amounts of time and energy, as in the creation of the class book. The salient features are that joint productive activities require students to talk and work with each other on a product that is meaningful and leads to growth. The teacher is present to support students' development.

Joint activities can easily be implemented through the use of classroom learning centers, which are a series of different activities that occur simultaneously in the classroom. For example, one history teacher uses learning centers to teach students about the major world wars.[2] As you walk into his class, students are clustered in small groups, each working on a specific task related to one of the unit themes, such as the political, social, and economic ramifications of war. Learning centers allow teachers to create diversified learning experiences within a curricular unit. (The full implementation of learning centers is discussed in Appendix 1.)

Research Support for Joint Productive Activities

Provided that essential elements are in place, a number of research studies in K–12 classrooms, in very diverse settings and across many content areas, have shown that students engaged in joint productive activities (or cooperative learning groups) consistently benefit. They have higher academic test scores, greater comprehension of the content and skills they are studying, higher self-esteem, larger numbers of positive social skills, and fewer stereotypes of persons from different races or ethnic groups.[3]

When researchers Springer, Stanne, and Donovan analyzed collaborative, small-group instruction in math and science undergraduate college courses, they saw remarkable improvements in academic achievement, attitudes toward learning, and perseverance through college programs. They recommended the widespread implementation of this type of teaching.[4] It is no surprise, then, that several programs and models listed in the U.S. Secretary of Education's *High School Leadership Summit* emphasize cooperative learning projects, Socratic questioning between teachers and students, and collaborative, project-based learning activities.[5] Clearly, incorporating joint activities into classes is not only a service to our students but a gift to society.

Research on cooperative learning consistently demonstrates positive academic and social gains. August and Hakuta report that students who participate cross-racially increase their academic achievement, motivation, self-esteem, and empathic development.[6] Kagan notes, "The lowest achieving students and minority students in general benefit most, but the benefit obtained for the lower achievers is not bought at the expense of the higher achievers; the high achieving students generally perform as well or better in cooperative classrooms than they do in traditional classrooms." Kagan further purports that improvements in ethnic relations were greater than any other outcome. Thus, the research points to the importance of incorporating joint activities into the curriculum.[7]

Working with Adolescents

Frequently teachers complain, "Let's be honest. Many of my high school kids hate working together. They are always fighting about something or with someone." It is true that joint productive activities can be fraught with conflict. All of life, in fact, can be full of conflict. One of the goals of joint productive activities is to encourage students to do what they do naturally outside the classroom walls: socialize, discuss, argue, agree, and arrive at resolution. Provided teachers have a clear, consistent classroom management system in place, students react positively and with much enthusiasm to joint activities (collaborative learning experiences). They especially appreciate the autonomy, the in-depth exploration of the subject matter, and the opportunity to work through different media such as the arts.

(For a more thorough discussion of management issues, see Appendix 1.)

During the 1998–2000 school years, at several northern California high schools, approximately 150 students in eight different classes were asked to complete a survey about their experiences with joint activities. Sometimes the activities were whole-group projects; other times, students were participating in small-group projects or engaged in learning center work. Overwhelmingly, the majority of students surveyed felt that they were learning about "real" things. As they made connections to their own lives, learning became more meaningful to them. In one survey form, a student commented, "I noticed people having conversations about the subjects and actually putting some intelligent thought into it!"

The students seemed to be connecting with each other and the material. When reflecting about a joint activity on slavery during the Civil War, a student wrote, "What I liked about this activity was the feeling the readings gave you. They described the slaves' feelings about how they were being treated. We actually discussed and imagined how we would feel if we were being treated like that. It wasn't just like reading my homework anymore. We're talking about people and their lives here."

The teachers of these classes began to experiment with collaborative activities and learning centers in order to increase student participation and motivation. As one teacher explains, they wanted to make school meaningful for their students. Teachers become enamored with joint activities when they observe students engaging in the activities: "When we saw Laura's students actually doing the activities, discussing the ideas, and coming up with thoughtful solutions to complex environmental problems, we were sold.

We decided to immediately revisit our next unit, reduce the time we spent lecturing, and increase the time students would be working on a project. The results are consistently gratifying. Students are turning in better work, asking thoughtful questions, and connecting with the material in a more engaged way. We feel like they are here, ready to work and be challenged."[8]

Creating Lessons with Joint Activities

In order to have successful joint productive activities, it is critical to have specific elements in place. Many teachers assume that they merely provide the directions and materials and then are able to spend some time grading homework papers while students work. This is a false assumption. In a joint productive activity, the teacher has a critical role and is integral to the learning process. The teacher is both a collaborator and a facilitator. The teacher acts more like a coach than a lecturer. However, since the teacher knows the material well, she becomes a valuable resource for the different groups.

For students to be successful at joint productive activities, they need the teacher to answer questions, clarify directions, offer content expertise, help mediate problems or conflicts, and model appropriate social and academic behaviors. The students can provide modeling and content knowledge for each other as well. However, they will only be able to take each other to a certain level of understanding and knowledge. It is the teacher who can often take them one step further into uncharted, unexplored territories of learning.

The teacher needs to introduce the students to the activity by clarifying the goals. Often the difference between a successful lesson and an unsuccessful one is the presence of a clearly defined goal and tangible learning objectives. Students must believe the work that they are doing is meaningful and relevant to their lives. They must have access to clearly defined instructions, know how the groups will be chosen, understand how they are going to be evaluated both as a group and as individuals, and be accountable for a debriefing or reflecting on the content and process of their work.[9]

The following elements are necessary for structuring successful joint activities:

- The teacher is present as a collaborator and facilitator.
- There is a clear goal with specific learning objectives.
- The product or project is meaningful and relevant.
- Instructions are clearly defined.
- Both individuals and groups have access to assessments.

By using *focus questions,* which serve as a guide to design, analyze, and evaluate activities, teachers can reflect on lessons that incorporate joint activities:[10]

Joint Activity Focus Questions

1. What is the goal of the lesson within the thematic unit?

2. How are the students co-constructing a product and sharing responsibility in the process? What is each student's part? What is the teacher's part? What is the co-constructed product?

3. What role does conversation or dialogue play? What academic language and concepts are students expected to use as they work?

4. What new knowledge and skills are students acquiring?

5. What changes could be made to make the lesson stronger and more meaningful?

Teachers can easily identify if they have defined a clear goal, requested a meaningful product, and required the application of academic language. They can also reflect on changes they might make to the lesson to increase its complexity or relevance.

Assessment of Joint Activities

The options for assessment of joint activities are vast and flexible; the key issue for teachers is to think about their goals and expectations, both academic and social, before beginning a unit. Teachers can use everything from journal entries to class presentations to end-of-unit tests to assess their students' knowledge of the new material. In addition, they can require students to use the newly acquired academic language in their written work.

Many teachers associate collaborative activities with undisciplined, loud, chaotic, unstructured instruction where students spend most of their time socializing with one another. In fact, joint productive activities require clear structures and procedures as well as defined learning objectives. If a teacher is concerned about what the students are learning in joint activities, the objectives can be assessed regularly by incorporating individual quizzes and exams into the unit. Throughout the chapter, different examples are provided.

Introduction to Laura Ianacone Taschek

Laura Ianacone Taschek is a high school teacher in Virginia. We met while she was completing her master's/credential program at a university in the San Francisco Bay Area. She was inspired to learn about the five principles outlined in this book and then committed to applying these principles to her teaching. Throughout the book, she provides examples from her own teaching that illustrate how to use the principles as a framework for crafting lessons as well as a tool for lesson analysis and self-reflection.

Laura has been teaching social science since 1997. She teaches a variety of classes, including world history, world geography, global issues, and freshman studies. Throughout her career, she has been inspired by a variety of teachers in the classroom. Some offered small, successful cooperative grouping strategies where students had real conversations and truly learned. Others used a more traditional whole-group approach, inspiring students with stories and interactive discussions. She states, "What I noticed about the latter was that these incredible conversations occurred with only a few of the students—those comfortable enough to pursue a discussion in a whole-group setting. The complacent, quiet, or beginning English Language Learner didn't participate with enthusiasm or deeply discuss the subject at hand."

Laura pondered how she could create an environment where her students were inspired and motivated to learn for themselves, for the good of humanity, and not just for the grade. She continues:

> In my Global Issues classes, there are limitless possibilities for topics: war, peace, international cooperation, and human rights—important life topics. But my students for the most part were unenthused, accomplishing only the minimum work required. Where was the enthusiasm? Why didn't my students share my excitement? The students pursued their schoolwork and participated in classroom discussions in a mechanical fashion. How can I reach my students' various learning and motivation levels?

These questions about teaching and learning brought Laura to a central question— "How can I make learning more meaningful to my students?"—which sparked a conversation that initiated the first joint activities and learning centers in her classroom. Learning center activities, based on a thematic unit, provide a successful format for implementing the five principles. Joint activities and learning centers offer students choice and flexibility. Students can work with their peers to determine the time line, focus of study, and solutions to complex problems. Laura testifies:

> The majority of my students look forward to the joint activities that are challenging, demand participation and sharing, tap into their experiences and knowledge, and teach academic concepts in a rigorous yet meaningful manner. They find them interesting and fun. They really enjoy working with their peers. The only complaint has been from a small, select group of students who find fault "with having to work and think." They state up front that they like to lay back and do nothing while the teacher talks. I believe the most effective instruction I can provide is to blend both joint activities in learning centers and direct instruction through mini-lectures.

So even during her lectures, Laura weaves in joint activities such as pair share. She discusses an important point and then turns to her students and asks them, with a partner, to discuss a pertinent question or concept.

Lessons from the Classroom

The following exemplary lessons illustrate how three different teachers designed and implemented joint productive activities in their classes. In the first lesson, students are asked to work in small groups to create a graphic organizer comparing and contrasting the author's use of figurative language to portray the setting in three pieces of literature. The second lesson requires students to work in teams to create an imaginary island that is geologically sound. This science lesson also asks students to reflect on their product as well as their team conduct. The final lesson occurs in Laura's world history class. Within the learning center structure, students design a castle. Then they are asked to evaluate what castles reveal about the political, economic, and cultural climate of the Middle Ages.

Lesson 1: Literature, Grade 10

Elva Hernandez has been teaching literature classes in the San Francisco Bay Area at Fairmont High School for the past decade. She enjoys doing group projects with her students because "it gives students the opportunity to use each other's expertise. They take pride in the completed projects whether they are literary analyses, letters to the author, or graphic organizers." She uses the joint activity focus questions to guide her planning and implementation of the lesson. Notice as you review this lesson how she has specific goals and the expectation for a clearly defined product that requires students to use the academic language of literary analysis.

Lesson: Time, Sequence, and Setting in Literature

Time Estimate: Two 53-minute class periods

Standards for Literary Response and Analysis

- Analyze and trace an author's development of time and sequence, including the use of complex literary devices such as foreshadowing and flashbacks.
- Recognize and understand the significance of various literary devices, including figurative language.[11]

Learning Objectives

1. Students will categorize the times, sequences, and settings of the following literature selections: *The Adventures of Huckleberry Finn* by Mark Twain, *Their Eyes Were Watching God* by Zora Neale Hurston, and *Ironman* by Chris Crutcher.[12] They will create a graphic organizer to arrange their ideas.

2. Students will analyze and evaluate how the author uses figurative language and symbolism to depict the setting.

3. Students will analyze how the setting deeply affects the plot and characters. How would the story have been different in a different setting?

Lesson Plan

1. In small groups of three or four, students work together to brainstorm the time, sequence, and settings of the literature selections.

2. The students create a graphic organizer, such as a chart, indicating the time frame, sequence, and type of environment in which the story takes place.

3. The students categorize their ideas.

4. The students discuss and take notes in order to analyze how the author uses figurative language and symbolism to depict the settings.

5. The students evaluate the effectiveness of the author's use of figurative language by discussing and taking notes about the following questions:

    *   What was most effective?
    *   Why do you think it was effective?
    *   What didn't work?
    *   Why wasn't it effective?

6. Students analyze how the setting affects the plot and characters. They discuss the following question and take notes: How would the story have been changed if the setting was different?

7. Next steps: After participating in the discussions and taking notes, students will write an essay. The essay will (1) document their ideas about the effectiveness of the author's use of figurative language to depict the setting and (2) evaluate the importance of the setting to the plot in each of these stories.

Conduct of Lesson

During the lesson, Elva rotates around the groups, answering questions, asking essential questions, solving a conflict, adding her own ideas, and prompting groups to think more deeply about their categories. There are a lot of open discussions and brainstorming of ideas. One group of students quickly gets to work categorizing their ideas as "Positive Features of the Setting" and "Negative Features of the Setting." Elva prompts them by requesting they consider the complexity of the three books. After discussing the similarities and differences in the stories, the group adds a category: "How the Characters' Lives Would Be Altered by a Change of Setting."

Commentary on Lesson

Elva comments, "Many students who would never dare raise their hand to speak in a whole-group lecture speak eloquently, clearly communicating their ideas to their peers." The students are required to collaborate, communicate, and work as a team. Every student brings an interesting perspective and contribution. Once the students start generating ideas, they seem to bounce off each other as the ideas take on a life of their own. One idea sparks another idea, which ignites a new discovery. By working together and sharing their individual thoughts and perspectives, the students end up thinking about ideas that they would not have had if they had been working alone. The groups created complex, sophisticated categories such as "How the Sequence of Events Affects the Characters' Behavior," "Community Interventions to Clean Up the Environment," "How Time Is Portrayed with Flashbacks," and "Global Responsibilities for Creating Healthy Settings."

Elva expresses her gratitude at having the joint activity focus questions to use as a framework for creating her lessons: "I am a believer in collaborative work. However, by using the focus questions, I know I am using a better format to create my lessons. Now I consistently consider what I want my students to learn: the goals and objectives, product or project, the academic language, and the new concepts."

Lesson 2: Biology, Grade 9

This lesson was created by Jeffrey, a high school science teacher who has been incorporating joint productive activities and project-based learning into his science classes for several years. He features this activity as part of a year-long "Community and the Environment" unit. Jeffrey consistently has clear goals specifically related to standards-driven, academic content material.

Lesson: Create an Island

Time Estimate: Two days of 90-minute block periods

Standard in Biology

- Have students create an ecosystem and then explore how the stability in an ecosystem is a balance between competing effects.[13]

Learning Objectives

1. Students will collaborate to create an ecosystem.
2. Students will identify the factors that affect the distribution and characteristics of the ecosystem.

Lesson Plan

1. In introducing the activity to students, explain that the goal is to create an ecosystem.
2. Students draw an island (using colored pencils and paper) and then identify the factors that affect the distribution and characteristics of the ecosystem.
3. Provide a couple of examples of things that could affect an ecosystem, such as changing weather patterns or the introduction of a new species to the island.
4. Explain that the class will be broken into groups of four and that each person will be responsible for one quadrant of the group's island map.

5. The team must work together because the map has to fit together seamlessly. For example, is there to be a river on the island? You cannot have a river simply end in one quadrant. The river would have an impact on the geography and the distribution of resources in the other three quadrants.

6. Pass out the instructions in Handout 1.1, "Create an Island."[14]

7. The students self-select into groups of four.

8. The students reflect on the final product and their process in working together by using reflection questions, which are set out in Handout 1.2. They discuss the questions in their group and then write a report individually.

Conduct of Lesson

When I observed this activity in Jeffrey's classroom, the students immediately started shifting tables, moving chairs, and gathering paper, pencils, and colored pencils. A low murmur was heard throughout the room. The students began. Jeffrey helped sort out materials. He rotated around the room until every group had an idea of where they were headed. In one group, a couple of the students started sketching out a plan. But another student in that same group starting erasing what one student was drawing, stating emphatically, "We have to talk first! You guys, we can't just start drawing. We don't even know what we're doing!" There was a lot of bickering, drawing, erasing, and loud complaining: "Cut it out! Let me draw." "I wanna get this done!" "No, we need to talk first!" The person sketching tried to explain that she had a clear vision of the ecosystem. She just wanted to get started so that they could get the work done quickly. She had an after-school job and had to work until 11:00 P.M. She would not be able to do any homework after school. Another student chimed in, reminding her that the task would take longer if they did not talk first. He also clarified with Jeffrey that they had at least two days to complete the project and the reflection writing. Jeffrey pulled up a chair and listened intently. After everyone seemed to calm down, he occasionally asked a question or clarified a student's idea.

The other groups were not as wrought with conflict. Snippets of discussion revolved around placements of geographical features and populations of species as well as how possible fluctuations in population size would affect the terrain and energy pyramid. At the end of the ninety-minute joint activity, Jeffrey asked students to sit together, reflecting and taking notes about how their work was going.

Lesson Assessment

Students are assessed on their final products as well as the reflection questions in Handout 1.2. At the end of the project, Jeffrey administers a quiz testing students about salient vocabulary and concepts and requiring them to provide examples from their joint activity.

Handout 1.1
Create an Island: Student Instructions

Biology Standard and Learning Goal: "To create an Ecosystem"

- Explain the factors that affect the distribution and characteristics of an ecosystem.

- Analyze the diversity and productivity of an ecosystem.

Following this project, we will be doing research to explain the factors that affect the distribution and characteristics of our ecosystem. We will also analyze its diversity and productivity.

Instructions

In order to begin this study, we will be constructing (in groups of four) an island and all of its major geographical features.

Conditions: Read BEFORE you begin!

- Your island as a whole must contain at least one of each of the following perimeter features: an isthmus, a bay, a gulf, breakaway isles, a peninsula, and an inlet.

- Your island as a whole must contain at least one of each of the following geographical features: mountains, volcano, forest, lake, marsh, river, and a waterfall.

- You must distribute the population and natural resources according to the geographical features.

- Your map as a whole must contain: a compass rose, a key (for size and features), and the island's name.

- You may add any other features your entire group agrees to, if you wish.

Now follow these steps:

Step One: Put yourselves into groups of four people.

Step Two: Each person takes a piece of paper and a black pencil.

Step Three: Decide among yourselves who will be responsible for each quadrant of your island. One person can draw or be mainly responsible for the northwest quadrant, one person can draw or be mainly responsible for the northeast quadrant, and so on.

Step Four: Figure out a way to make sure that your perimeters will meet each other's correctly when you assemble your four quadrants together. Then assemble your island together (using tape on the back). Perimeters must meet precisely.

Step Five: Using colored pencils, add all of the required geographical features and map requirements to your island map.

The representation of the geographical features must be realistic, and they must coordinate (for example, rivers cannot flow uphill, marshes must have water, a river must have a source). Also, remember that geographical features do not limit themselves by quadrants. Coordinate with your group to have your features cross over your artificial lines.

Remember to coordinate your key so that you all use the same symbols and colors to mean the same things.

All members must agree to the island name. You must reach consensus.

Handout 1.2
Create an Island: Reflection Questions

- Describe your finished product. What are the most salient features of your ecosystem?

- Pick one feature of your ecosystem, and explain its impact on the geography and distribution of resources.

- What do you think are the most important factors that affect the characteristics of our ecosystem in our local area? What do you think are our local diversity and productivity?

- How do you think your team worked together? Please address what really worked well and what you could have done differently to make the process run better.

- Please write about your contribution and explain an issue you had to negotiate with your peer(s).

Jeffrey wants the students to be forced to communicate about how to make an island and consider the factors that affect the distribution and characteristics of an ecosystem. This is why he asks each person to complete only one quadrant. He is concerned about the issue of accountability. This activity blends group work with individual accountability. Using the "Create an Island" reflection questions, he requires the students to write about their contribution and state what issues they had to negotiate with their peers. For example, if they started building a mountain range in their quadrant, they had to discuss how the mountain would affect the island's ecosystem. How would this affect the stability of the producers and decomposers in the other quadrants? Jeffrey selects his joint activities carefully so that the product is created by the group, but students can be individually assessed and held individually responsible for their contribution.

Commentary on Lesson

Students learn more about ecosystems in the joint activity than they could have in a more conventional format. In a traditional lesson, students more than likely would listen to these important ideas presented in a lecture format. Later they would be tested on the material.

Within this joint productive activity, however, students engage in discussing their ideas, arguing about placement of geographical features, complaining about each other's placement of a mountain range or an isthmus because of the way it affects the terrain as well as population. They talk about salient features of their ecosystems, describe the distribution of resources, and predict what affects their own local ecosystem. In addition to memorizing the vocabulary for the test, they have to apply it in their writing and use it in their discussions.

Jeffrey comments, "An improvement to the lesson would have been to blend this activity with a more traditional lecture so that students would have more information to work with when they create their islands." Through a lecture that integrates a collaborative strategy such as pair share, students would have more data to apply to the construction of their ecosystem.

Lesson 3: World History, Grade 10

Laura Ianacone Taschek created the following activity as part of a Middle Ages unit in her tenth-grade world history class. In addition to teaching the unit through mini-lectures, she cycles students through various learning centers focusing on aspects of medieval European society and culture. At one of the centers, students watch a video about castles and are then given a set of questions to discuss collectively and answer individually. They are then involved in a collaborative castle-building activity, including development of a "defense plan" for the castle.

Lesson: Castle Building, Middle Ages Unit

Time Estimate: Four to five 60-minute class periods

World History Standards

- Students learn about the redefinition of European society and culture, 1000–1300 c.e.[15]

Learning Objectives

Students will be able to construct a castle and connect it to significant themes of the Middle Ages such as survival, war, the emergence and assimilation of different cultures, the rise of religion and its consequences, changing political systems, economic evolution, and artistic developments.

Lesson Plan

1. Students will view a video on castles and respond to the Castle Questions (Handout 1.3). They discuss the questions and responses as a team. Then each member writes up his or her own responses.

2. In their small groups, students design and construct a castle either out of actual building materials or as a sketch, using a computer drawing program or pen and paper (Handout 1.4).

3. The team creates a defense plan for their castle integrating concepts from the video as well as text and Internet resources.

Conduct of Lesson

Laura comments that she listens to students talk and work together as they begin the joint activity. She is impressed that they use newly learned knowledge of castle construction. They apply vocabulary to describe the parts of the castle, assist each other in the correct placement of castle parts, and describe how the construction of the castles added to the defense strategies. Using what they see in the castle video, with additional help from library books, the students reconstruct castles, with not only the towers, walls and courtyards, but also the murder holes and other specifically designed defense strategies. For an example of student work, see Appendix 2.

Consider this discussion among five students working on building a castle:

Student 1: What are we supposed to do?

Student 2: I dunno.

Student 3: I'll reread the directions. Listen this time!

Student 4: We have to draw it out first.

Student 2: I'd rather build it, then draw it.

Student 5: I think I did this in seventh grade. Do we really have to do this?

Student 3: Let's sketch it, then build it. Look, there are these books here. John, YOU check them out!

Handout 1.3
Castle Questions

Castles

As the era of the Middle Ages was wrought with conflict and change, there were many wars and battles that raged throughout the land. People began to build castles to house their families and servants and to protect them against the ever-changing enemy.

The first castles consisted of a motte and a bailey, the motte being a large conical mound with a flat top and the bailey being the land that was enclosed by a ditch (preferably filled with water). Entrance to the bailey was gained via a strongly defended gate and bridge that ran over the ditch (moat). There was also a tower that housed the owner, his family, and servants. It was frequently the last line of defense. The castles that we think of and see today were built up from the original motte and bailey timber design. Over time, stone replaced the timber. Much attention was given to the design and construction of the tower, the protective walls or enclosures, and the gatehouse for security purposes.

Part I

In your small group (of no more than four students), watch the video on castles and take notes by answering the following Castle Questions. Please discuss the questions collectively, but each person must submit his or her own answer sheet.

Castle Questions

1. Summarize the original castle design and construction.

2. Explain how it evolved from the early design to the sophisticated stone edifices that we see today in Europe.

3. Summarize the defense features.

4. Analyze in detail how these castles, which were built of stone, were subject to attack. What were the different strategies?

5. Please judge the strengths and challenges of these castles as structures of defense. How would you design them differently?

6. Compare this early military system to our system today.

7. Determine what castles reveal to us about the Middle Ages. What stories do they tell us about the life and times of the people: the political, economic, cultural, and religious climate?

8. How do the Middle Ages compare to the times we live in today?

Handout 1.4
Castle-Building Activity

Part II

1. Congratulations! You all have just been named lords and will soon begin building a castle. Unlike the architects of the Middle Ages, you have had the benefit of learning about more than one style of castle construction and defense before you begin to build. Using what you have seen and read, do *one* of the following:

   - As a group, *draw a detailed illustration of your own castle.* You should include the surrounding fief in your drawing. Label the sections of the castle, interior and exterior. Identify and label the sections of your castle that will protect you and your fiefdom from an attack. If needed, replay sections of the video or use the resources listed below.

   - As a group, *build a castle.* You should include the surrounding fief in your plan. Label the sections of the castle, interior and exterior. Identify and label the sections of your castle that will protect you and your fiefdom from an attack. If needed, replay sections of the video or use the resources listed below.

2. You are creating a miniature castle. Please establish a scale, and draw or build your castle accordingly. You will have access to the following materials: cardboard, poster board, glue, scissors, tape (masking and clear), markers, and acrylic paint. If needed, you may supply other materials. I suggest planning your design so that it takes no more than two or three class periods to complete the drawing or construction.

3. As a group or pair, write a one-page defense plan should your castle come under attack. Include terms you learned during the video/book work. How will you defend your castle against invaders?

4. Upon completion of your castle, the class will be voting on the best castle construction (including apparent defense strategies).

Good luck!

Resources

Gravett, C. (2000). *The Middle Ages* (Vol. 1). New York: Longman

Gravett, C., & Dann, G. (2004). *Castle.* New York: DK Publishing

http://www.castlewales.com/casterms.html

http://www.britannia

In the dialogue that follows, the students identify where the gates should be placed and why. They share their knowledge with each other through discussing and showing each other their ideas. They seem to be enjoying the project, each adding special touches and drawings to accompany the model castle. A few students explore the option to use computers to complete their projects.

Teacher: What's working?

Student 1: Learning how to work well in groups.

Teacher: How so?

Student 1: We are learning how to build a castle, and then we have to build one as a group. We are all working on different parts of the castle.

Student 2: We've got walls over here and archer rooms. I didn't know much about archer rooms; they figured out how to use angles so they wouldn't be shot at. Cool.

Student 3: We have a problem. The gate is not supposed to go all the way through; it is supposed to go around.

Student 4: It goes right underneath it.

Student 5: What it is . . . is the gate on the outside needs to be offset from the gate on the inside.

Student 3: That was so the attackers couldn't get right in; they had to go around.

Student 4: Like this one.

Student 2: No, it has to be the gate into here. So once the attackers got past the first gate defense, they had to do it again.

Student 5: Oh, that makes sense.

Student 1: Hey, who was fighting who? I don't really even know.

Student 2: One of us should look that up. I'll do it on the computer. It'll add to our design.

Student 3: I can do it at home on my dad's computer.

Student 5: Whatever. I think we should have something about who's fighting who now.

Student 1: What are you talking about?

Student 5: Duh—like this year. Like, have we been fighting about the same stuff since then?

Student 1: No, they fought about land.

Student 5: Oh yeah, like there aren't wars about land now?! Duh.

Student 3: Ms. Taschek, you want us to think about now, yeah?

Teacher: Yes, I like where you are headed. We do all fight about land. Could the issues have been similar for the people of the Middle Ages?

Lesson Assessment

Laura uses two primary forms of assessment during joint productive activities. First, she observes. She walks around, interacting with the students and asking questions about what they are doing. She states:

> I never forget the extremely social nature of the high school experience. When other teachers have observed my class, the most popular question they ask is: Are the students staying on task? I explain that I carry a clipboard with a class list. I jot down notes about who is doing what, who is on task, and who needs more support and guidance. I also jot down questions, insights, and reflections that arise. I make a point to talk to students individually.

The other way she ensures that students are staying on task is by implementing a second form of assessment. The day she passes out the information about center activities, she also passes out a rubric that explains to the students exactly what she expects of them and how they will be graded (Exhibit 1.1). The students are clear from the beginning about the goals and expectations for completing commendable work and participating in an exemplary manner.

Commentary on Lesson

Laura has students consider the following questions:

- What stories do castles tell us about the life and times of the people of the Middle Ages?
- How do the Middle Ages compare to the times we live in today?

By working with each other, students draw conclusions, make comparisons, create hypotheses, and build off each other's ideas. Laura wants her students to recognize that history unfolds as a series of tales of survival and adaptation. As one group of students concludes, "When you look at the negative aspects of our world—wars, economic problems, and religious persecution, and the positive aspects such as universities and the arts—the Middle Ages doesn't look that different from how life is today."

EXHIBIT 1.1. ASSESSMENT RUBRIC FOR THE CASTLE ACTIVITY

1. **Participation:** 50 points possible. This grade includes your participation in pairs or small groups while working on the centers in class. It also includes how much time you spent on task/activity (actually doing the task/activities) during the center work in class.

   50 points = always participating and working on task/activities
   40 points = frequently participating and working on task/activities
   30 points = moderately participating and working on task/activities
   20 points = occasionally participating and working on task/activities
   10 points = hardly participating or working on task/activities

2. **Activity/Task Work:** Total points possible (6 × 50) = 300 points
   50 points = Work reflects thoughtful, well-developed, and insightful answers. Summarized, clarified, or discussed the questions in each task/activity. When asked, provided examples from the text or your own life. Completed all sections of the task/activity. When asked, created excellent drawings, illustrations, or visuals for task/activity work. (As a group, each member contributed, which means there are full, complete answers for each question and a quality illustration. Don't rush your work. Don't forget to include all group members' names!)

   40 points = Briefer summary of main points/limited or short discussion of questions. Included some examples from the text and your own life. Illustrations or visuals included in task/activity work.

   30 points = Minimal response to questions in task/activity (one sentence or less). No illustrations completed.

   15 points = Task/activity incomplete. Only some of the questions are answered. No visuals or illustrations provided.

   0 points = Task/activity not complete.

3. **Presentation:** 30 points possible. Upon completion of the center work, small groups will prepare and present their work. (more details soon)

   Remember: EVERY POINT COUNTS!

   Total points possible: 380 points

   Total points: _____

Conclusion

Within the past two centuries, our economy has moved from an agricultural to an industrial to a global, technological, information management one. As teachers, we must prepare our students to deal with the onslaught of information and the ever-changing structures and systems within our interdependent world. Within the workplace, we must be able to work effectively in teams, solving complex problems that cannot be worked out alone. We live in the era of specialization. Each person is required to provide a piece of the solution. This requires cooperative collaboration.

The rate at which information is being processed has rapidly accelerated. This requires that students develop a different set of skills than they needed a decade ago. They used to memorize facts about a specific subject, be tested on their knowledge, and then receive a grade for their performance on a test. Now, by the time students complete the class and take the exam, the scientific or mathematical knowledge has been further developed and published. Questions such as "Why is this important to know?" "How do we know this to be true?" "How did we arrive at this conclusion?" and "What is the proof for this mathematical concept?" have become increasingly important. It has become critical for students to know the subject matter, effectively communicate their ideas, work as a team, make consensual decisions, and respect each person's knowledge and expertise. By integrating collaborative learning or joint activities into the classroom, we are providing our students with opportunities to practice communicating effectively, negotiating complex problems, and resolving conflicts.

Reflecting on the economic, political, and social milieu of our society demands that we commit to providing students with experiences in collaborative, cooperative learning. We want them to leave high school prepared with deep subject matter knowledge, an ability to reflect on their understanding and how they have come to know what they know, and strength in working cooperatively and peacefully with family members, peers, and coworkers.

Developing Language and Literacy Across the Curriculum

The way a person functions linguistically is such an integral part of self that it cannot be separated from the health and well-being of the person. . . . Any theory or practice of literacy teaching [must] take into account the deep and powerful implications of language in the whole personality.

Don Holdaway, *The Foundations of Literacy* (1979)

Enacting the principle of language development means that teachers are committed to creating lessons that teach students the important concepts and vocabulary so they can understand the essential subject matter. Consequently, when students read the material, they understand what they are reading. As teachers, how often have we read through state mandates or personal legal documentation that we clearly could not understand because we did not have prior knowledge of the subject or familiarity with the terms, symbols, and other vocabulary being used? How many times have we thrown up our hands in frustration? How can we support our students to learn academic material in ways that they understand and make sense to them? As Lev Vygotsky states, "Language is a primary vehicle for intellectual development. Language is not only a means for communicating information, it is also an important vehicle for helping learners broaden and deepen their understandings."[1]

Dalton notes, "Whether in bilingual or monolingual programs, whether instruction is in English, Spanish, Navajo, Zuni, or Chinese, language and literacy development in the language(s) of instruction are the foundation for teaching and learning. The foundation is laid by creating interactive contexts where students can participate in language and literacy activities. . . . Students must have the opportunity to engage in *purposeful* conversations both with their peers and the teacher."[2]

We must teach content, but more important, we must teach our students to be literate human beings. We want to help them develop competence in the different languages and subjects of school instruction, whether it is in mathematics, science, social science, music, art, or literature. Our goal is twofold. We want to assist them in becoming proficient at using and applying academic English so that they may be successful students. Simultaneously, we want to prepare them to be thoughtful and highly functional citizens who possess the capacity for reasoning, problem solving, weighing options, and making clear judgments about personal, family, community, and world issues.

The following questions assist teachers in recognizing if they are enacting the principle of language development. Teachers use the questions to design, analyze, and critique activities. The focus questions can be used as a guide to reflect on a lesson and make changes to how we teach the concept:[3]

Language Development Focus Questions

1. **How are you developing students' language of the subject area by incorporating reading, writing, speaking, and listening activities into the lesson?**

2. **How are you requiring students to use and apply the content vocabulary?**

3. **How are you eliciting, restating, and clarifying subject matter content in meaningful conversation and writing with your students?**

4. **How are the activity and the expectations being modeled by you or students?**

5. **What types of questions are you asking? How are they requiring students to use higher-level thinking processes such as analysis, evaluation, and synthesis?**

Scaffolding Instruction

In addition to focus questions, it is important to consider how we scaffold instruction. Scaffolded instruction means that "every piece of information learned and every skill acquired provides the next-level substructure for building higher-order knowledge."[4] Scaffolding is the process by which the teacher models how to think about an idea or complete an activity. Gradually the teacher turns the thinking process and work over to the student, who thereby assumes more responsibility for completing the activity independently. Among possible scaffolding strategies are these:[5]

- Showing students a model of the assignment

- Providing an example of what the finished product might look like

- Interviewing students about what they already know about a subject

- Helping students make connections between and across concepts that might appear unrelated

- Fostering self-assessment through reflection questions

- Providing student interaction and discussion time

Lessons from the Classroom

The following lessons illustrate how three teachers approach integrating the principle of language development into a math, science, and language lesson. Traditionally, math and science teachers have not thought of themselves as language teachers. Beth, a high school math teacher, comments, "I couldn't possibly teach English. I have always excelled at math and science. Honestly, I don't even read, never been a reader. I always bombed out on the standardized tests in reading." In lesson 1, we get to observe how Beth uses the language development focus questions to guide her teaching in ways that incorporate language teaching into her geometry lesson. In a similar manner, Brian crafts a vocabulary lesson around core science concepts in lesson 2. Sara, a high school literature teacher featured in lesson 3, has expanded her career due to demographic changes in the school's population and teaches classes for English Language Learners. All three teachers use scaffolding strategies in their lesson plans. In addition, they all recognize the importance of teaching language, vocabulary, and the accompanying conceptual ideas in order for students to make sense of the academic material.

Lesson 1: Geometry, Grade 9 or 10

Beth created this lesson in response to her frustration with her students' performance on a geometry exam. After tabulating the exam results, she interviewed a couple of students about their performance. Several suggested that they needed some concrete experience to learn about angles and what difference angles could possibly make in the world. One complained, "How are we supposed to learn and remember this stuff: isosceles, hypotenuse, acute?" The frequently asked question "Why do we have to know this stuff anyway?" comes up repeatedly.

Beth's initial lesson included only lecture and a textbook assignment where the students solve problems. But she is aware of the limitations of lecture: "I was losing them during the lecture. The glazed-over look. The head-down-on-the-desk. I wanted them to be more engaged, to speak to each other about possible solutions and listen to each other's ideas."

Beth then decided to offer students an opportunity to work with triangles and angles in a real-world context. She wants them "to experience the language by speaking it, listening to their peers speak it, working with it through building a tent, writing labels for the angles, and providing proofs to support their construction." She comments, "Without knowing the vocabulary and understanding the basic concepts of geometry, students hit an impasse. They must know the basics to go on to learn trigonometry. I never thought of myself as a language teacher, but I realize that I am teaching language—the language of mathematics." Beth recognizes that students need to know how they will be evaluated on a hands-on math project so she creates a rubric that clearly clarifies her expectations.

Lesson: Geometry Construction

Time Estimate: Two or three 60-minute class periods

Mathematics Standard

- Students develop their visual and spatial reasoning to construct formal, logical arguments and proofs in geometric settings and problems.[6]

Learning Objectives

1. Students will be able to identify and define the basic facts, terminology, and theorems about the triangle.

2. Students will be able to apply their knowledge by designing and constructing a serviceable tent using material and pole rods.

3. Students will label and measure the angles as well as the perimeter and area of the tent.

4. Students will write an analysis and provide proofs of why certain angles can support weight.

Lesson Plan

1. Deliver mini-lecture defining the important vocabulary about triangles and geometric angles.

2. Have students complete the textbook exercise for homework. Give in-class time as well.

3. In class, students work in groups of three or four to design and construct a serviceable tent. Students have the option of constructing miniature tents or full-size ones if the materials are available. For miniature tents, provide students with the following materials: rulers and tape measures, protractors, poster board (or some other sturdy type of cardboard), and masking and electrical tape. For full-size tents, provide students with the following materials: rulers and tape measures, protractors, cloth (nylon or cotton), doll rods, and masking and electrical tape.

4. Students are responsible for giving a brief presentation of their tents to their peers. They are required to label and measure all angles, perimeter, and area. They must also provide proofs that illustrate why certain angles can hold weight and others are unable to support weight.

5. Students hypothesize how this simple construction activity could apply to architecture—the construction of buildings. For example, most buildings are rectangular in shape. How do construction experts strengthen the building? How does this compare to our work building tents?

6. Move around the class observing student work and discussion. Encourage students to use the geometric terms by modeling them frequently as you discuss the tents, and answer and ask questions as appropriate.

Lesson Conduct

While students build their tents, Beth walks around the class, giving advice when necessary, clarifying what an angle is called, discussing its measurement, modeling the vocabulary, and asking questions that require students to analyze their work. She asks, "Why is a triangle more stable than a rectangle? How can you prove it? What angles form your tent? How can we compute the centroids of the various triangles of your tent?"

Lesson Assessment

Beth uses the rubric provided in Exhibit 2.1 to evaluate her students' performance with the tent activity. She explains that she takes notes about her students' performance as she moves throughout the room so that she can give them a score for Part II of the rubric.

Revised Lesson

After initially revising this lesson by adding a hands-on math project, the tent-building activity, and the rubric, Beth recognized that she loses some of her students' attention during the mini-lecture. Thinking about her students' divergent learning styles and using the language development focus questions, she decided to add a pair share component to the lecture: "I add a piece to my mini-lecture where every five minutes or so, after every new concept and vocabulary item, I have the students work in pairs to solve a problem related to the concept I just taught." Item 1 in the lesson plan is then revised (the addition is italicized):

1. Deliver mini-lecture defining the important vocabulary about triangles and geometric angles. *Stop during the lecture to have students in pairs complete problems that illustrate the concepts. For example, after defining the classifications of triangles, have students, in pairs, work together to label several examples.*

EXHIBIT 2.1. RUBRIC FOR TENT CONSTRUCTION ACTIVITY

I. Construction of Tent Using Geometric Language and Thinking
   A. Clearly delineated tent design; tent itself is strong and stable; accurately labeled triangles and angles; mathematical proofs provided to support construction using geometric vocabulary and conceptual terms.
   B. Rough sketch of tent design is provided; tent is standing; some triangles and angles are labeled; some mathematical proofs are provided to support construction using a minimal amount of geometric vocabulary and conceptual terms.
   C. Minimal or no sketch of tent design is provided; tent is wobbly (at best); lack of accurate labeling of triangles and angles; lack of mathematical proofs.

II. Process of Construction and Academic Discussion
   A. Group works cooperatively to construct tent: Uses important vocabulary when discussing the design and construction; listens to each other's ideas; participates equitably to create labels and mathematical proofs.
   B. Group constructs tent: Uses some vocabulary when discussing the design and construction; listens minimally to each other's ideas; creates labels and mathematical proofs.
   C. Group constructs tent without cooperation or discussion; little evidence of listening to each other's ideas; minimally labeled; no mathematical proofs provided. (In this case, each individual will have to redo the assignment.)

Beth then makes a second change to this lesson. Instead of being the only one to evaluate her students' knowledge and performance, she asks students to weigh in as well and gives them these instructions:

1. **Use the rubric to complete a self-evaluation by rating yourselves and writing a brief synopsis of how you thought you performed on the tent activity.**

2. **Document what you think that you have learned about triangles and angles.**

3. **Rate and briefly comment on your team's work.**

Beth is pleased and surprised about the students' responses to the changes she makes to the lesson. She comments, "They are talking and helping each other solve problems. They seem more engaged with the material. I still have a few kids on the outside who are not really participating. But the majority are talking. In fact, they are talking so much that they are now giving me feedback about things I don't really want to hear about [laughs]." Beth feels that the biggest success is the change she has made to the lecture: "This is something I will use all the time now. Even though it takes longer to deliver the information, I see that they are getting it—or not getting it. They are more engaged with the content. They seem more interested during these lectures— less passive and more involved."

Beth's lesson illustrates that language is a key component to mathematics lessons. She demonstrates how language is embedded and can be amplified in an average lesson. Students move from being passive recipients of information to active collaborators in discussing, constructing, and applying a mathematical concept.

Lesson 2: Earth Sciences, Grade 10 or 11

This lesson was created by Brian, a high school science teacher who teaches in a rural part of the Midwest. He recognizes the importance of teaching students the necessary vocabulary so that they can understand the core academic concepts. In this lesson, he uses a literacy strategy to enrich the language aspect of the lesson while teaching core science content. The literacy strategy is a graphic organizer called a *word web*. Brian uses the word *web* to strengthen language acquisition. It requires students to see the semantic associations of words and categorize the vocabulary and concepts in meaningful groupings. Word webs demand that students think about the ideas and their relationships to one another.

Lesson: Plate Tectonics Language Activity

Time Estimate: Approximately one week of 90-minute class periods

Science and Technology Standards

- Students should (1) understand how plate tectonics operating over geologic time have changed the patterns of land, sea, and mountains on Earth's surface. (2) Use technological tools to advance learning.[7]

Word Web

When teacher and students collaborate to construct a list of their ideas about a specific topic, they can use a word web (also known as a semantic web, brainstorm web, or mind map). Usually the topic idea is written in the center of a chart paper. Other ideas, concepts, or categories that relate to the main topic are written around the central word. Lines are usually drawn to connect the satellite words to the central word. This activity is used to document students' ideas about a particular topic. It provides one way of thinking about and organizing information. It also requires the learner to see the relationship among conceptual ideas. With high school students, it is important to teach them to record their ideas in categories and not simply as random ideas. This makes the work more cognitively challenging. We are pushing our students to evaluate and sort their ideas into larger conceptual pieces.

Learning Objectives

1. Students will define vocabulary terms that are necessary for learning about the study of plate tectonics.

2. Students will create a word web to demonstrate knowledge about the organization and conceptual framework of the content.

3. Working in small groups or pairs, students will create a Web page (if the school has the necessary online resources) or computer-generated report that illustrates their knowledge of plate tectonics and the occurrence of earthquakes.

Lesson Plan

1. Post photographs or illustrations of the earth and its layers, a map illustrating the different plates, and scales used to measure earthquakes on the classroom walls or whiteboard or chalkboard. Also post a piece of paper or chart paper next to each picture. You can download pictures off the Internet. Keep them simple. Laminate them so you don't have to gather them the next time you teach this unit.

2. Ask students to walk around the room and write down any vocabulary, information, or observations they make about the pictures on the paper next to the picture.

3. Ask students to walk around the room one more time to see what their peers have written next to the pictures.

4. In small groups of three or four, students conduct book and Internet research to create a word web documenting what they are learning about plate tectonics. Give them Handouts 2.1 and 2.2. Students may write their ideas on sentence strips for organizing material into categories on chart paper.

5. In their same small groups, students will create a Web page or computer report about the topic.

Handout 2.1
Plate Tectonics Word Web Activity

1. With your small group, you will be constructing a word web about plate tectonics.

2. Read the word web description on the word web handout [Handout 2.2].

3. You will be doing preliminary book and Internet research to find out all you can about plate tectonics. You will add these ideas to your word web. Remember to record questions that come up as you do your research.

The Challenges

- You must record your ideas in categories and not simply as random, unrelated ideas. So, please organize your ideas.

- You must record all the important vocabulary that you discover. Make sure you understand what the terms mean, or you will get stuck during your Internet and book research.

- Include a section of questions on your word web. Some of these questions can form the basis of your research work. For example, you might want to know why and how the continental drift and sea-floor spreading theories changed when geologists discovered the existence and movement of the plates. Or you might want to know more about the 2004 tsunami that killed so many people and wiped out several islands in the Pacific. How could we have prevented such a tragedy?

4. After completing your word web along with your questions, you will now conduct research with your same small group to address your questions and expand your knowledge base. You will be creating a web page that illustrates your research in an innovative, interesting, and scientifically accurate manner.

Handout 2.2
What's a Word Web?

A word web is a collaboration of your group (with contributions from your teacher). You will construct a list of ideas about a specific topic. In this case, the topic is plate tectonics.

Usually the topic idea is written in the center of a chart paper. Other ideas, concepts, or categories that relate to the main topic are written around the central word. This activity is used to document your ideas about a particular topic. It provides one way of thinking and organizing information.

You will use sentence strips to record your ideas. Sentence strips are long, thin pieces of chart or poster board paper that can hold a sentence or two. By writing the ideas on sentence strips, you can move them around to different categories. Simply put tape on the back of them and attach them to the chart paper. Move them around until you find categories that fit together and make sense. Connect your ideas to the central word with lines.

Conduct of Lesson

During the first part of the lesson, students walk among the posters, writing down phrases and words, shrugging their shoulders at times, chatting about the illustrations. Sometimes Brian and his students become disheartened when they realize how little they know about the topic. At other times, they get excited about the growth they inevitably make over time.

Quickly they break into small groups, grab the student handouts, and pick up a piece of chart paper. They begin to jot down notes about plate tectonics. Many groups have a separate paper for their questions. Three groups gather at the computers to begin doing Internet research. The other groups begin looking in class textbooks for information. One group asks to go to the library. Brian gives them permission but also requires them to return within a half-hour and show him what they find.

Commentary on Lesson

In this lesson, Brian states, the language serves as the foundation for students' understanding. Without knowing and being able to explain the terminology and the basic concepts, the students are limited in their ability to analyze why an earthquake happens, hypothesize the reasons for the 2004 tsunami, and evaluate how we might become better able to predict and prepare for earthquakes.

Word webs are a valuable tool in that they help students brainstorm about different topics. However, it is critical to challenge students to think in complex and challenging ways. Determining categories and subcategories requires students to develop a schema: synthesizing, analyzing, and evaluating larger pieces of data into a workable, organized framework.

Brian wants his students to work in groups so that they use the vocabulary to discuss the concepts. He comments, "Being a science teacher, I have my students do a lot of reading and a fair amount of writing—writing up lab reports, answering essay questions. But I had to look at how I was asking them to talk with each other. I really wasn't. That's why I started having them work more in groups. Real scientists discuss ideas and brainstorm solutions to problems together. I wanted to simulate that type of environment in my classroom—at least some of the time." Brian also works with the groups to model using the terminology; ask guiding and clarifying questions; explain misunderstandings; and pose pertinent, analytical, or evaluative questions.

Lesson 3: Sheltered English, Grades 9 to 12

Sara teaches Sheltered English Instruction (SEI) classes for English Language Learners.[8] Sheltered English is a set of linguistic, instructional, assessment, and classroom-management practices that teachers use with English Language Learners from all levels (advanced to beginner) to develop content-area knowledge, skills, and increased language proficiency.[9] In her SEI classes, Sara does her best to provide modified instruction in English without oversimplifying the material. She is working with her students to read expository (nonfiction) text. It is critical to give students who are learning English (or any other language, for that matter) as many visual aids and experiential learning opportunities as possible, including realia (the objects or activities used to relate classroom teaching to real life) and models of exemplary work. However, as Sara states, "Problems arise if we stop there—just as if we only give decontextualized text to language learners. I strive to offer a balanced curriculum of visuals, experiences, and text." The conceptual underpinnings are laid out within text. If students are unable to access the vocabulary, they will not be able to access the concepts embedded within the text.

Lesson: Expository Reading Activity

Time Estimate: 60 to 90 minutes

Standards for English Language Development

- Read expository material and analyze how clarity is affected by patterns of organization, repetition of key ideas, syntax, and word choice.[10]

Learning Objectives

Students read several articles, write a report clarifying what they learned about a specific food, and analyze how the authors got their message across using the organization of key ideas and vocabulary choices.

Lesson Plan

1. Students divide into small groups of four or five people each.
2. Each group will read a different article about a food. They also get a copy of Handout 2.3.
3. They will write a list of all the words that describe the specific food according to the article they read and the pictures they viewed.
4. Each group gets a sample of the food they are studying.
5. After eating the food, the students make additions to their list of words that describe their experience.
6. Individually, they write an essay about a different food. They can follow the organizational framework from the article they just read.

Handout 2.3
The Properties of Food

1. Readings and Discussion
    - Read the reference article.
    - After you've finished reading, take three to five minutes to talk with your partners and create a list of words that describes your food. How does it look, feel, smell, and taste?

2. Line Drawing of Your Food
    - Brainstorm as many words as you can to describe the food based on the drawing. Do this with your partners.

3. The Real Food!
    - Examine your food very carefully. With your partners, talk about what you see and sense. Brainstorm words that describe the appearance, feel, and smell of your food. Make this list with your partners. Use all the language that comes to mind. Describe and note the words, sensations, and associated thoughts that come into your mind.
    - Eat the food. Record the words that come to mind as you eat.

Conduct of Lesson

As Sara met with different groups, she heard conversation where beginning English Learners were using words like *phytochemicals* and *flavonoids* to describe the health properties of apples. In a group reading about grapes, the students were discussing the article using vocabulary such as *cordon, can,* and *node.* Exhibit 2.2 shows the word lists from a group that read about oranges, analyzed a photo, and then examined and ate an orange.

EXHIBIT 2.2. SAMPLE OF STUDENT WORK FOR EXPOSITORY READING

ARTICLE

Sweet	*Grow lots of places*	*Ovular*
Leaves glossy	*Abundant*	*Thick*
Have small white flowers	*Round*	*Yellowish*
Pale yellow	*Sugary*	
Juicy vesicles	*Protruding navel*	
Could be dry!		

PHOTOGRAPH

Fruit	*Round*	*Smooth*
Leafy on the inside	*Orangish*	
Juicy on the inside	*Disk-like*	
Small 2-inch diameter		
Looks different on the inside than on the outside		

ORANGE

Juicy	*Orange*	*Rough*
Thick skin	*Squirts*	*Bumpy*
Yellowish	*Green spots*	*Textured*
Knobby	*Smells bitter*	*Thick*
Smells sweet	*Citrusy*	*Sticky*
Squirts a spray	*Leathery*	*Tart*
Sweet taste	*White skin*	*Rough*
Like a grapefruit or lemon		
Little pods that contain juice		
"Smells fresh, like spring"		

Sara had this to say about the lesson: "I really think it is important to have the text. I can see how the picture and the experience are good, but my kids wouldn't have access to the academic language without the text. Phrases like, '. . . which under favorable conditions may yield fruit for 60 years or more. The pungent leaves have a glossy, wax-coated surface. The small white flowers, which are borne in clusters . . .' and so on. My kids would never say things like that to each other. 'Pungent leaves.' 'Borne in clusters.' 'Phytochemicals.' They don't talk like that! At high school, they need the text, and I need the text to do my job."

Commentary on Lesson

This activity provides an example of how to weave students' everyday understandings into academic language. For example, students were using the word *juicy* frequently to describe certain fruits. As Sara worked with different groups of students, she asked them to practice using the technical terms. Instead of saying *juicy,* she would model using the words *juice vesicles* or *juice sacs.* She asked students to practice using this vocabulary and required them to use it in their writing. By practicing the new vocabulary, students have a context for understanding the use of these words. Instead of repeatedly hearing the word *smelly,* they could learn to use the term *pungent.* Enacting the standard of language development requires that we give our students access to the language, specifically content vocabulary, so that they can express their ideas in an academically rigorous manner.

Lesson 4: Global Studies, Grades 11 and 12

Using the California State Standards, Laura Ianacone Taschek focuses on teaching current, science-based, societal topics in her Global Issues class. She reflects on how she gets students involved in discussing the subject matter with each other: "There are no opportunities for them to talk to each other about the ideas. It is the same old dilemma about lecture. I think the information I am giving them is critical to understanding the most pressing environmental issues at this point in our history. However, I can't make them listen. And we all know that they tune us out if they are not interested in the subject. For me, this is one of the hardest parts of teaching: feeling that I am losing them, knowing they don't care about really important phenomena that I am passionate about." Laura wants to change this. She recognizes that students need opportunities to talk to and listen to each other.

There are two versions of Laura's lesson plan here. The first is a more conventional plan and the second an improved version. Using the language development focus questions, Laura enriches the lesson by modeling the activity, increasing the opportunities for students to talk and work with each other, and having students prepare and present a PowerPoint presentation of their ideas.

Lesson: Examining the Environment

Time Estimate: One 60-minute class period

Science Content Standards

- Students will investigate a science-based societal issue by researching the literature, analyzing data, and communicating the findings.[11]

Lesson Plan

1. In a mini-lecture, give a brief description of the most pressing global environmental issues: biodiversity, genetic engineering of food, human population, global warming, animal and nature conservation, waste and pollution. Write these topics on the board.

2. Tell students to choose a quote from *Save the Earth* by Jonathan Porritt and write a one-page (or longer) response to the quotation, including their own personal opinion about what concerns the author has brought up.[12] They should relate it to their own life and own global environmental concerns. How does this quote relate to them? How does this quote relate to one of the topics on the board?

———————————————

Commentary on Lesson

Laura decides to involve her students by first having them talk with each other about the quotation. She creates guiding questions so that the students have a clear idea of the expectations for their work with a partner. She admits, "I am very concerned about their discussions being fruitless and unproductive. A colleague of mine suggested that I start by having students do a quick write, which takes only three to five minutes."

A **quick write** is a literacy strategy meant to stimulate reflection about a subject.[13] We provide students with a short, open-ended prompt such as, 'How does this relate to your own life?' Students write a brief response to help them reflect on the subject and begin to organize their thoughts and questions. Laura sees that it is an effective way to help students think about and organize their thoughts before sharing their ideas. She decides to have students do a quick write, reflecting on and answering the questions from the original lesson plan individually and then sharing the information with a peer. She also adds a research project that pairs students in preparing a PowerPoint presentation.

Laura examines how she is modeling the activity and her expectations: "I see that I do little, if any, modeling. I only elicit answers to questions during my lecture. If a student happens to ask a question during the lecture, which is very rare, only then do I clarify or elaborate on the subject. In my classes, conversations happen before class starts and begin again after class is over. The conversation never revolves around the subject we are studying."

To incorporate some modeling, Laura decides to incorporate a **think-aloud.** She picks one of the quotations from the handout and models thinking out loud why she picked the quotation—how it was meaningful to her. Think-alouds require students and the teacher to talk about what they are thinking, doing, and understanding about the subject. They can also report the feelings they are experiencing as they read a text or complete an activity.

Laura realizes quickly that the reason that many students do not use content vocabulary in their essays is that she has never explicitly required them to do so: "I just assumed that when we study something, students would use core vocabulary in answering the questions. I realize that I must make vocabulary requirements explicit."

Laura evaluates whether the questions require students to engage in higher-level thinking processes such as analysis, evaluation, and synthesis. She feels secure about having students evaluate the problem in relation to their own lives and asks, "How does this problem affect you? How is it meaningful to you in your daily life?" Laura comments, "Basically, I can see that the lesson is pretty standard: listen to the lecture, and then do an activity showing me that you understand some of the information. I am going to improve it by shortening the lecture, allowing much more student interaction, and expanding the assignment to make it more collaborative and meaningful." Laura's new, revised lesson plan follows below.

Revised Lesson: Examining the Environment

Time Estimate: Approximately six 60-minute class periods

Science Content Standards

- Students will investigate a science-based societal issue by researching the literature, analyzing data, and communicating the findings.

Learning Objectives

1. Students will choose one of the important or essential ideas that are affecting our global community and research the topic to identify the problems and possible solutions.[14]
2. Students will delineate how the topic affects our daily lives and interactions.
3. Students (in partnership) will deliver an interactive PowerPoint presentation about their topic.

Lesson Plan

1. Write these major topics on the board: Biodiversity, Genetic Engineering of Food, Human Population, Global Warming, Animal and Nature Conservation, Waste and Pollution. Tell students that these are the big ideas we will be studying for the next six days.

2. Write the following Robert Redford quote on the board and model a think-aloud: **"What we are living with is the result of human choices and it can be changed by making better, wiser choices."**[15] Then model a think-aloud: "I chose Robert Redford's quote because I like what it says about our future. Often it is easy to be overwhelmed by all the environmental problems in the world, but to me, the quote represents hope. I actually think of this quote every time I throw out something that I know I could recycle. I know if we all started recycling everything that we could, the amount of waste, of garbage, of pollution, we have would be reduced by 30 percent, according to the latest statistics from our local waste management company."

3. Ask students to read selected quotes and complete the quick-write activity on Handout 2.4. Students may pair up first.

4. Ask students to conduct a more extended research project working with a different partner. They are to pick one of the big ideas noted on the board and may spend up to three days preparing a PowerPoint presentation on the topic as described in Handout 2.5.

5. Test students at the end of the unit by asking them to analyze two quotes from *Save the Earth* and write an essay in which they provide a detailed summary of the global environmental problem as well as possible solutions.

Lesson Assessment

Laura explains that she assesses her students by giving them an end-of-the-lesson essay exam as described in the last part of Handout 2.5. In addition, she gives students a rubric before they begin the assignment so that they know what the academic expectations are and how they are being evaluated. Laura uses the rubric for grading literary responses in Exhibit 2.3 as a framework for creating rubrics that fit her assignments.

Commentary on Lesson

Laura finds the language development focus questions extremely useful in helping her evaluate lessons. She moves the responsibility for delivering the information in a lecture format to her students by having them research the topics and prepare an interactive PowerPoint presentation. She reaches her goals of shortening her lecture, allowing student interaction, and expanding the assignment to make it more meaningful. In addition, she incorporates some modeling and, through the PowerPoint presentation, requires students to use and apply key science terms appropriately. She is providing students with opportunities to develop and use, speak, read, write, and listen to scientific language in several different contexts.

Handout 2.4
Quick-Write Activity

1. The book *Save the Earth* is filled with meaningful quotations by different artists, writers, politicians, and activists. Please select one quotation, and complete a quick-write answering the following questions:

   - Describe what the author is saying.

   - How does the author's message bear on your own life? How is his or her experience or opinion similar to your own ideas?

   - How would you revise the quote to make it most meaningful to you?

2. Share your quick-write ideas with your partner.

Handout 2.5
Research Tasks for PowerPoint Presentation

Please choose a different person to work with. Pick one of the big idea topics on the board. You and your partner will spend three days in the library doing computer research on your big idea. You are required to do a PowerPoint presentation for your classmates on the topic that meets the following criteria:

1. Provide a detailed description of the topic.

2. List the three most important problems.

3. Provide a possible solution to each of the problems.

4. How does this topic affect our own lives on a daily basis (even if we are not aware of it)?

• Your presentation must be interactive. This means you must have your peers engaged in some kind of meaningful conversation or activity about the topic. Examples include pair share, creating graphic organizers, or watching and responding to a video clip.

• I will be circulating from group to group to check your work. I will be available to answer questions and discuss the information.

• You will sign up for a fifteen-minute time slot on Friday to give your presentation.

• Your test at the end of the unit will be to analyze two quotations from *Save the Earth* and provide a detailed summary of the global environmental problem as well as possible solutions. You are responsible for listening, taking notes, and studying these topics. (By the way, one of the quotations will be about the topic that you did your presentation on!)

EXHIBIT 2.3. RUBRIC FOR GRADING LITERARY RESPONSES: ENVIRONMENT UNIT

You will be evaluated on the quality of writing as well as your understanding and presentation of the content.

Stellar! = A

A. You address each aspect of the question and explain, analyze, and/or critique key concepts.

B. You provide clear explanations and understandings of key concepts from the readings and class discussions. You seamlessly weave in core content vocabulary.

C. You demonstrate a *developed* understanding of the main themes/topics and the ability to relate and make insightful connections among (1) the readings and class discussions, (2) your observations and experiences, (3) your own educational experiences, and (4) other relevant teaching and learning experiences.

D. You supply *more than one vivid and clear* description, instructional example, or anecdote that is well integrated with key concepts.

E. You carefully select *quotes* from readings, literature, or concepts from other courses to elaborate your understanding of questions raised.

F. You demonstrate accurate and consistent standard writing conventions including grammar, usage, punctuation, capitalization, and spelling. The accurate use of writing conventions as well as the organizational structure and presentation *consistently* enhance the readability of your paper.

OPTIONAL: You may use visual diagrams, graphic organizers, word webs, or other formats that illuminate relationships among key concepts and personal experiences.

Well Done! = B

A. You address each aspect of the question and explain, analyze, and/or critique key concepts.

B. You provide clear explanations and understandings of key concepts from the readings and class discussions. You weave in core content vocabulary.

C. You demonstrate a *developing* understanding of the main themes/topics and the ability to relate and make *insightful connections between two of the following:* (1) the readings and class discussions, (2) your observations and experiences, (3) your own educational experiences, and (4) other relevant teaching and learning experiences.

D. You supply *one vivid and clear* description, instructional example, or anecdote that is well integrated with key concepts.

E. You carefully select *one* quote from readings, literature, or concepts from other courses to elaborate your understanding of questions raised.

F. You demonstrate accurate and consistent standard writing conventions including grammar, usage, punctuation, capitalization, and spelling. The accurate use of writing conventions as well as the organizational structure and presentation *usually* enhance the readability of your paper.

OPTIONAL: You may use visual diagrams, graphic organizers, word webs, or other formats that illuminate relationships among key concepts and personal experiences.

Satisfactory! = C

A. You could address each aspect of the question and explain, analyze, and/or critique key concepts with *more detail and clarity.*

B. You demonstrate an understanding of the main themes/topics and the ability to relate and make *one insightful connection between two of the following with minimal detail:* (1) the readings and class discussions, (2) your observations and experiences, (3) your own educational experiences, and (4) other relevant teaching and learning experiences.

C. You supply *one vivid and clear* description, instructional example, or anecdote that is well integrated with key concepts. You weave in core content vocabulary.

D. You demonstrate a *developing use* of standard writing conventions including grammar, usage, punctuation, capitalization, and spelling. At times, inaccurate use of writing conventions as well as the organizational structure and presentation *interfere with the readability* of your paper.

OPTIONAL: You may use visual diagrams, graphic organizers, word webs, or other formats that illuminate relationships among key concepts and personal experiences.

Please Revise! = F

A. You *did not address* each aspect of the question and explain, analyze, and/or critique key concepts. Your explanations are cursory, vague, or superficial.

B. You *did not demonstrate* an understanding of the main themes/topics and the ability to relate and make *one insightful connection between two of the following with minimal detail:* (1) the readings and class discussions, (2) your observations and experiences, (3) your own educational experiences, and (4) other relevant teaching and learning experiences.

C. You *do not supply* one vivid and clear description, instructional example, or anecdote that is well integrated with key concepts. You do not weave in core content vocabulary.

D. You *do not demonstrate* a developing use of standard writing conventions including grammar, usage, punctuation, capitalization, and spelling. The errors distract the reader and make your paper difficult to read. You *need to do extensive editing* on the text. You also demonstrate inaccurate use of writing conventions as well as organizational structure.

Note: If you have received a "Please Revise," your paper may be revised and resubmitted for further feedback until you and the teacher are satisfied with your work.

Note: In this text, the writing rubric has been changed from its original form. It was originally created in collaboration with Susan Freeman in fall 1998. The term *Stellar* was originally introduced to me by Andrea Whittaker and Susan Freeman.

Conclusion

In all four exemplary lessons, the teachers move from being solely core subject matter experts to being language teachers as well as content experts. They are recognizing the importance of providing students with the language tools—syntactical understandings and conceptual knowledge—to be able to navigate through the content. The teachers recognize the importance of providing students with many opportunities to use language in a variety of forms.

Teaching vocabulary is more than giving students a list of terms and requiring them to write definitions and an accompanying sentence. Teaching vocabulary is a complex process that encompasses teaching students to recognize, construct, and articulate the relationships among terms, meanings, and concepts. The teaching of vocabulary must be linked to language, math, science, and social science curriculum.

Teachers serve as gatekeepers. We have considerable control over students' access to higher education and different arenas of academic experience. If we do not prepare them with a strong foundation in academic language, we limit their choices as well as access to social and economic opportunities. Our job is to be the assistants in students' life-long pursuit of learning. Language and literacy are at the heart of that learning.

Contextualization or Making Meaning
Connecting School to Students' Lives

3

> *Students' histories often remain masked—sometimes through the student's choice, sometimes by the overwhelming demands of teaching, and sometimes by the teacher's choice. . . . Every student has a history, and that history affects every facet of who they are and how they learn. . . . If we do not hear them, we cannot hope to fully understand or teach the students in our care.*
>
> Ethan Mintz and John T. Yun, *The Complex World of Teaching* (1999)

It is the last period *of the school day. Amy, a high school art teacher in Chicago, asks her students to create a realistic painting using oil pastels. A student who recently moved to the city from southern Arizona is painting a sunset. Her colors are vibrant; the paper is aglow with rich ambers, deep violets, dabs of hot pink and neon orange. Some teachers might question the realism of the painting as it does not resemble Chicago's color schemes. But Amy inquires, "Tell me about when you have seen a sunset like this. How satisfied are you with the tone and hue? How do you like the Chicago sunsets as compared with the Arizona ones? What about Arizona do you miss?" She thus successfully begins a conversation with her student about her life and prior experiences.*

This vignette illustrates the importance of learning to listen to our students' ideas, experiences, and histories. It pinpoints the necessity of getting to know our students so that they stay interested in sharing their perceptions and opinions. To do this effectively, we ask questions of our students. We chat both formally (in our structured, academic, classroom settings) and informally with them as often as possible.

Contextualizing instruction in students' knowledge base gives teachers a springboard from which to jump. Instead of starting each lesson anew, we assess what our students already know from both their previous school, home life, and community experiences. Their experiences provide a reference point, a foundation, from which to begin our instruction. By building on what students' already know, we decrease the boredom factor that we hear about repeatedly throughout students' high school careers. By demonstrating an authentic interest in their thoughts and ideas, we decrease the feelings of invisibility that adolescents often experience.

Contextualizing instruction helps students learn by bridging what they already know to new material. Recently a friend began teaching social studies in the local high school that has a population close to 90 percent Mexican American. Being from a middle-class, Caucasian family, he was unfamiliar with Mexican cultural rituals and ceremonies. Several of his students were celebrating their *Quinceañera* during the year. He recognized that this Mexican American coming-of-age celebration was similar to his sister's "Sweet Sixteen" party. Translated by his students as "Sweet Fifteen Years," it carries a spiritual component of commemorating a child's arrival into "adulthood" through a church ceremony followed by a large party. Clearly the event carries social as well as religious significance.

He took a great interest in the students' enthusiasm and decided to learn as much as he could about this ritual. Because it is a large family celebration that can often be costly, he decided to incorporate a unit on budgeting and economics in his social studies class. The students were elated. They were eager to assist each other in planning a budget, comparing prices, and making important monetary decisions. After the unit, they commented, "We are really working on something that is important to us. Usually school is kinda boring. We get talked to a lot. The teacher talks and talks and talks. With this, I am learning something that I remember. I have something to share with *mi familia.*"

Contextualizing instruction makes a difference to students. It shows them that we are interested and care about them, their ideas, and their families. Students buy into curriculum that is meaningful to them.

Contextualizing Instruction Within the Community

In an ideal world, schools would be inextricably linked to their communities. This would make high schools places of learning as well as arenas for social action. Enid Lee describes the "social change stage," that is, "when the curriculum helps lead to changes outside of the school. We actually go out and change the nature of the community we live in. For example, kids might become involved in how the media portrays different people and start a letter-writing campaign about news that is negatively biased. Kids begin to see this as a responsibility that they have to change the world."[1]

Typically our social reality precludes the full integration of schooling and social action. There has been a growing movement to incorporate service-learning into schools throughout our nation. Service-learning makes certain that schools provide meaningful service to the community with curriculum-based learning.[2] However, operating a schoolwide service-learning program requires district grant funding. We are headed in a positive direction; however, a clear gap exists between schools and communities. In this chapter, I present ways to bridge the gap that usually separates the two. Enacting the principle of contextualization allows teachers to integrate students' home and community knowledge and expertise within classroom lessons. From parent interviews to researching and attending local environmental seminars, teachers can incorporate service-learning projects into their daily lesson plans.

Cultural Compatibility

Student populations today are diverse. Most high schools serve a multiplicity of cultures and communities. How do we represent our students' funds of knowledge with the diversity of cultural and linguistic understandings and experience? What is culturally and educationally meaningful to our body of students? While it is critical to get to know your students and tailor the curriculum to meet their needs and interests, it is important to expand their knowledge. The rich diversity of students allows teaching and learning to extend beyond what is familiar and comfortable.

Erma, a high school math teacher, recounted a story of a few high school students who were tutoring a group of elementary children. They were teaching them how to carry when they were doing double-digit addition:

$$
\begin{array}{r}
1 \\
16 \\
+\ 48 \\
\hline
64
\end{array}
$$

After modeling several problems, one second-grade student, Marie Luisa, raised her hand and firmly stated, "*Maestra,* this is not how we do adding in Mexico." And she proceeded to show how to do double-digit addition using the concept of place value:

$$
\begin{array}{r}
16 \\
+\ 48 \\
\hline
14 \\
+\ 50 \\
\hline
64
\end{array}
$$

Although the answer was the same, the process and the thinking involved in arriving at the answer was very different. Erma recounts that several children who had been struggling with the skill of double-digit addition understood Marie Luisa's way. The rich diversity offered by heterogeneous groups of students allows both teachers and students to grow beyond and enrich their familiar understandings and knowledge.

Research Support

The principle of contextualization as an important ingredient in the mixture of sound pedagogical practices is well documented throughout the standards movement. The National Council of Teachers of Mathematics and the National Science Standards encourage teachers to construct curriculum that draws on real-life problems and student and community values.[3] The International Reading Association supports teachers in building connections between literature and students' real-world experiences.[4] Research on English Language Learners states, "Prior knowledge plays a significant role in learning" and "studies incorporating into the classroom features of learning and talking that are characteristic of the homes and communities of English Language Learners have shown positive results."[5]

In addition to the support from the standards movement, the main theories of human development, including cognitive science, constructivism, and sociocultural theory, concur that the development of knowledge occurs by connecting new information to what is already known. Contextualizing instruction in students' previous experiences and understandings aids them in building schemata. Consequently, in reading instruction, the building of mental maps enhances comprehension and recall more than any other instructional strategy.[6]

Finally, students themselves provide testimonials clarifying the need for school to be meaningful and relate to their lives. In *Voices from the Inside,* they recount feelings of alienation and disenfranchisement with the educational system. They request the need for their knowledge and experiences from outside the school walls to be visible, represented, and validated.[7]

Contextualizing Lessons and Activities

In order to contextualize instruction successfully, it is critical to consider how the school curriculum makes a difference in students' lives. We have to ask ourselves, When are we allowing students to talk? How are we integrating participation structures such as pair shares or think-alouds so that student can be the experts and share their knowledge? How are we accessing their knowledge? Are we using informal interviews, formal interviews, essays, or oral presentations so that students have an opportunity to share their knowledge? And how are we assessing what they know so that we build on their knowledge base and not repeat what they already have learned? We must clearly define the goal of the lesson so that learning does not turn into therapy sessions of sharing past experiences but gets directly linked to academic goals.

On a more sophisticated, and difficult, note, how are we integrating family and community knowledge into our teaching? We must be realistic. The planning and logistics are time-consuming and often difficult, if not impossible, to implement with working parents, budget cuts, and adolescent cynicism. How do we connect to life outside the school walls? How do we bring family members into class as speakers? How do we arrange class excursions to places that are important to our studies? Examples of excursions teachers have arranged include a science teacher taking seniors to a local gardening project cared for by the homeless, another taking her class to an exhibit of famous African American writers at the local library, and a math teacher arranging a tour through a local technology company that hires student interns to work on specific Web-based projects. Community outreach often connects what students are learning in school to the greater community, providing a more meaningful context for learning about biodiversity, computer technology, or contemporary literature.

To make school more meaningful for students, we ask ourselves how we are connecting the school content and required state and national standards to their lives. When we are functioning as expert lecturers, often we forget to take a moment to ask students to reflect on how the material is relevant to them. How does the information expand their understandings? How does this knowledge get disseminated and applied within their home or community? The following focus questions assist teachers in linking lessons more deeply to students' lives:[8]

Contextualization Focus Questions for Planning Lessons

1. **How is this activity meaningful and connected to students' lives?**

2. **How are you creating opportunities for the students to talk about their own home and community lives and experiences?**

3. **How does the lesson provide opportunities for students to apply and expand on what they know and have just learned in school?**

4. **How are students' cultural preferences, such as style of conversation and participation, integrated into the activities?**

5. **How are members of the community, parents, and families integrated into the activities?**

Lessons from the Classroom

The lessons in this chapter provide examples of how different teachers strive to contextualize lessons in their students' prior experiences and knowledge. In the first lesson, Diane uses the novel *Farewell to Manzanar* to teach middle school students about the tragedies of war. She personalizes the book by having students participate in a role-play activity, comparing the characters' experiences to their own.[9] The second lesson is an activity that Monica uses with her ninth- and tenth-grade biology students. This activity, which can be applied to any content area, requires students to reveal what they already know about a subject and then build on that knowledge. In the last lesson, Laura Ianacone Taschek accesses students' understandings about culture and then takes them through several experiences to expand and broaden their knowledge.

Lesson 1: Language Arts/History, Grade 8

This activity is part of a larger unit designed to support the state language arts standard and develop students' ability to reflect on the themes of war and persecution, hatred, racial prejudice, and survival. It features role-play and writing exercises to support the teaching of *Farewell to Manzanar* by Jeanne Houston and James Houston. *Farewell to Manzanar* is a memoir about the internment of a Japanese American family during World War II. The lessons can be adapted for use with other works of literature featuring similar themes, such as *The Diary of Anne Frank* or *Desert Exile* by Yoshiko Uchida.[10] The lessons effectively illustrate how contextualization can make a work of literature more dramatic and meaningful.

Lesson: Tragedies of War: The Japanese Internment

Time Estimate: 40 minutes to 1 hour

Standards: Literary Response and Analysis for Grades 6 to 9

- Students read and respond to historically or culturally significant works of literature that reflect and enhance their studies of history and social science.
- Students clarify the ideas and connect them to other literary works.
- Students engage in expository critique by exploring instances of bias and stereotyping.[11]

Learning Objectives

Through a role-play and quick-write exercise, students will get a glimpse into the reality of the Japanese Americans during World War II who were forced to leave their homes and possessions and live in Japanese internment camps. They will reflect on, write about, and share their experiences with their peers, exploring the themes of hatred and racial prejudice, persecution, and survival.

Lesson Plan for Role Play

1. Prepare students for this lesson by sending a note home to parents and the students that briefly describes the activity. (A parent can refuse to have his or her child participate.)
2. Ask students to participate in role-play exercise:
   - Invite four to six students to volunteer as "guards" serving on behalf of the U.S. government, and tell the remaining students they are to imagine that they are comfortably at home. (It is not necessary for the other students to imagine that they are Japanese Americans since prejudice takes all forms. They can be just who they are and be subjected to the same treatment for a myriad of reasons, such as racial identity, ethnic background, socioeconomic class, gender or religious preference.)

- The guards are to "follow orders" and tell the other students to leave their homes immediately and that they have only two minutes to collect their belongings. No pets are allowed. The guards may shout, "Hurry up, pack quickly, come on, let's go," while their peers are trying to figure out what to take.

- The other students are given two minutes to write down what they would take along if they had to leave their homes immediately.

- The guards quickly escort everyone outside the classroom, where they are ordered to line up against the wall and wait for six to eight minutes.

3. After six to eight minutes, allow all students back into the room, and ask them to do a quick-write describing (1) how they felt during this experience and (2) another personal experience they had in which they felt threatened or had something taken away against their will. Both the "detainees" and the "guards" complete the quick-write. (See the examples in Exhibit 3.1.)

4. After they finish the quick-write, students do a pair share to exchange their stories. Each student takes a turn sharing his or her ideas either by reading what he or she wrote or simply retelling those ideas.

5. As a class, ask students to construct a list of words that describes how they felt during the exercise.

6. After studying *Farewell to Manzanar,* students will read *The Diary of Anne Frank* and compare the themes as well as the historical period of time of the two books.

EXHIBIT 3.1. EXAMPLES OF STUDENT QUICK-WRITES

Rachel's Quick-Write

I am Jewish and my dad always tells me that people hate Jewish people. I have to hear stories every year about WWII and what the Germans did to the Jews. I have even seen videos. They are disgusting to me and my brothers. I don't need to see that. It just gives me nightmares. Some nights, I do get scared. I get scared that the police will come and get me just like Anne Frank. I get scared about being Jewish. I don't tell many people. When they had us lined up against the wall, I got really scared. I thought maybe it was real. I didn't know we did this to Japanese people. There is something wrong with us.

Eddie's Quick-Write

I thought it was dumb. Nobody is gonna mess with me. I will beat em up to a pulp like in Pulp Fiction—blow em away. My older brother is always taking my stuff. I hate it. He will just waltz in and take whatever he likes—like my skateboard one day. I hate that. I hate it. What did those people do wrong where they took em away? Musta been something or other.

WORD LIST

Strange	*Uncomfortable*	*Sad*	*Weepy*
Foreign	*Itchy*	*Unfair*	*Panic Attack*
Scared	*Tired*	*Confused*	*Prejudice*
Terrified	*Fearful*		

Lesson Plan for Literary Analysis

1. Following the quick-write and the word list construction, give the students further background about the book or topic to be studied. In this case, students are told that they will be studying a book focusing on the period of time when all people of Japanese descent were sent away and put into internment camps in the northwestern and southwestern states. They had to depart quickly, leaving behind their beloved pets and precious possessions. Often family members were separated. Their experience was real and not a simulated one like what we just experienced.

2. Introduce the book. Students are required to maintain a literary journal where they augment the initial word list. They also must respond to writing prompts as we read the book:

   - How do you think this character felt?

   - How do their feelings compare to your own when you have been threatened (as in the previous activity) or had someone or something you love threatened?

   - Analyze a specific instance of bias and prejudice. Support your thinking with text references.

3. Next steps: (a) To meet the Literary Response and Analysis Standard, the students will read *The Diary of Anne Frank* and compare the salient features of both novels. (b) Invite speakers to talk about surviving both the Holocaust camps and the Japanese interment camps. Students prepare questions (with teacher supervision).

Commentary on Lesson

In analyzing this activity using the contextualization focus questions, we see that the lesson is effective in helping Diane's students see the relationship between their own lives and the experiences of Japanese Americans during the period of time portrayed in *Farewell to Manzanar*. In simulating the loss and grief of having to give up everything they knew and loved, Diane's goal was to develop empathy and compassion for the Japanese internees. As Diane indicates, "Contextualization is a finely tuned skill of connecting our students' experiences to academic standards." Through her essential questions, "How do you think this character felt? How do their feelings compare to your own?" Diane's lesson helps students weave their own experiences of loss with those of the characters in the text.

Using this instructional approach that includes contextualization, Diane boosts student motivation and engagement. Contextualized instruction honors and validates the experiences of students who have experienced injustice in their lives due to racism, classism, religious prejudice, or homophobia.

Diane uses this activity to enable students to examine the concept of hatred, a topic that has great meaning and relevance for adolescents, who are often concerned about injustice and feelings of powerlessness. She poses a number of questions: "How can we keep this type of hatred from developing again? What can we do as individuals to keep this type of hatred out of our lives? How do we deal with hatred on a personal level? What is buried beneath hatred?" Diane finds that many students are relieved to hear that everyone experiences feelings of hatred, just as they experience feelings of sadness, loneliness, and love. Having the opportunity to talk about their lives and feelings draws her students into discussions:

> Students who don't normally talk very much or write very much suddenly have a lot to say. And I mean a lot! Some of my students have come from Mexico; others from El Salvador where they have had to basically give up their whole life—their home, family, friends, everything that was familiar. They had to go through much transition and heartache for only being thirteen, fourteen, or fifteen years old. They understand fear, loneliness, and, unfortunately for some of them, hatred. It is revealing to have a forum to discuss their experiences and also a meaningful way to link their lives to other people's lives through literature, historical fiction, and nonfiction. I also use this unit as an opportunity to work on their writing. [Laughs] It's a great occasion to edit a piece of their writing and work on conventions as well as content. Their motivation is high because the subject is important and meaningful to them. My motivation is high to take advantage of their enthusiasm to teach them about history as well as subject-verb agreements!

Lesson 2: Biology, Grade 9 or 10

The following activity is a group collage project developed by Monica, a high school science teacher who teaches a Science and Social Action unit as part of her tenth-grade biology class. As she states, the unit is "a vehicle for students to attain a level of ecological literacy consistent with the state ecology science standards." She uses the collage project "to find out what my students know and build on their knowledge." The lesson is used as a tool to access what students already know about a subject from previous school or home knowledge. Then they graphically build on their knowledge base, adding pieces to the collage as the unit progresses.

In this lesson, Monica uses the project with groups of students. However, she also recommends having students complete individual collages. In this way, she can access what they have previously learned about the topic, view their development of knowledge over time, and assess what they have learned by the end of the unit. Monica has shared this lesson with other teachers who have taken the steps and adapted it to various content areas. She defines the instructions for the collage project in Handout 3.1.

Lesson: Collage Project

Time Estimate: 60 to 90 minutes

Ecology Science Standards

- Students know that biodiversity is the sum total of different kinds of organisms and is affected by alterations of habitats.
- Students know how to analyze changes in an ecosystem resulting from changes in climate, human activity, introduction of nonnative species, or changes in population size.[12]

Handout 3.1
Instructions for the Collage Project

1. In groups of four to six, you will create a collage using butcher paper, markers, magazine and newspaper clippings, scissors, tape, and colored pencils. You can use the computers to write up pieces of text you want to incorporate, including four to six questions that your team has about the topic.

2. Since you have only forty-five minutes, you must work quickly and efficiently.

3. Your goal is to create a collage that reflects everything you know and have experienced about biodiversity. Think about what you have learned about the topic from your family, friends, community, television or radio, Internet, and school. Remember to reflect on what questions you have about the topic and include those in the initial design of the collage. Also, save space to record your knowledge as we study the topic and your reflections at the end, noting what you have learned that is personally relevant to your life. Remember, you are also required to hypothesize how the biodiversity of a specific ecosystem has changed and possible solutions to repairing the damage if any has occurred.

4. Since you are under a time crunch, here is one possible suggestion for time management:
   - 15 minutes: Every member looks through magazines and newspapers and cuts out anything that relates to his or her past experiences.
   - 15 minutes: Every member writes text that also explains or describes his or her past experiences and questions or concerns he or she wants addressed in the unit.
   - 15 minutes: Tape or glue everything together in an aesthetically pleasing manner!

5. Presenter: During this process, make sure that you talk about your experiences and knowledge. You will need to choose one member to present this piece of the collage and share this information in five minutes or less.

6. Timekeeper: You will definitely want to appoint a timekeeper since you are under a time crunch.

7. Before the member of your group presents your collage, you will also be participating in a brief "gallery walk" so that you have an opportunity to look at everyone's work.

Assessment

8. Please refer to the Collage Project Rubric [Exhibit 3.2] so that you know how you are being assessed. Please note that you are being assessed on your group participation as well as the quality of your thinking.

EXHIBIT 3.2. COLLAGE PROJECT RUBRIC

A: Excellent—Outstanding
B: Very Good—Above Average
C: Average—Okay
D: Needs Improvement—Unsatisfactory

I. Product and Reflection

A. The student(s) explored several options, generated ideas, built ideas off prior knowledge, and discussed ideas if appropriate to the assignment. The work reflects the students' thinking processes. The collage is visually exciting and original.

B. The student(s) created the work from one idea instead of exploring options. Visually the collage is well done.

C. The student(s)' work reflects minimal thoughtfulness and originality. The collage is adequate. It would have benefited from more effort.

D. The student(s)' work reflects a lack of thoughtfulness and originality.

II. Hypothesis About Biodiversity

A. The students included a section of the collage that illustrates the relevance of human interaction on the biodiversity of the ecosystem. They have *thoroughly* examined the resulting damage; hypothesized/explained the reasons for the destruction; and constructed/researched *creative* and *thoughtful* solutions for repairing the situation.

B. The students included a section of the collage that illustrates the relevance of human interaction on the biodiversity of the ecosystem. They have examined the resulting damage; hypothesized the reasons for the destruction; and constructed/researched at least one solution for repairing the situation.

C. The student(s)' work reflects minimal effort in including a section that illustrates the relevance of human interaction on the biodiversity of the ecosystem.

D. The student(s) did not include a section that illustrates the relevance of human interaction on the biodiversity of the ecosystem.

III. Group Work

A. The student worked very effectively in the group. He or she was committed to clearly communicating ideas, participating in collaborative decisions, listening to other students' perspectives and reasoning, working toward achieving group goals, and completing his or her share of the work.

B. The student worked effectively, communicating ideas and assisting in the decision-making process.

C. The student did an adequate portion of the work. He or she participated minimally in the group process.

D. The student participated minimally in the group work and process.

Learning Objectives

1. Students will define biodiversity.

2. Students will analyze the effects of climatic changes, human activity, and interventions on the biodiversity of ecosystems.

3. Students will hypothesize how the biodiversity of a specific ecosystem has changed and possible solutions to repairing the damage if any has occurred.

Lesson Plan

1. Goal: Students will work as a team to construct a part of a collage that represents what they know about biodiversity. They pick a specific area to represent, such as the forest, woodlands, wetlands, or prairie. The collage can include photos, other graphic illustrations, and text. In addition to accessing their initial knowledge base, students must record questions they have that they want addressed throughout the study.

2. Initially, as a class, you can brainstorm (a) the biodiversity of different ecosystems and (b) salient terms that they might want to include in their collage.

3. After completing this initial piece of the collage, students will add to it as they gain more information and develop insights into the topic of biodiversity.

4. Finally, students will complete the collage by adding a section of the most important things they have learned about the topic. In addition, each group of students will be focusing on the biodiversity of a specific ecosystem. They will hypothesize how the biodiversity has been affected by human intervention. They will design possible solutions to repairing the damage if any has occurred.

Commentary on Lesson

Through this introductory activity, Monica is trying to get students to access what they already know about the subject. She explains:

> I suffered a certain amount of boredom in high school. I felt detached from the material and as if my teachers did not care that I already studied this subject last year—and the year before that. Not that I remembered it! But I remembered not caring very much. I want students to get involved. I want them to know that I realize they might know something about biodiversity.
>
> Because I live with a fifth-grade teacher, I know they study habitats in elementary school. So they've been exposed to forests, wetlands, grasslands, and prairies. My job is to figure out what they know and build on to that base. My job is also to figure how to make this meaningful to them. That is why I insist that they include questions on their collage. Who cares about biodiversity? What does it mean? How might it be really important to our lives and our families—whether they live here in northern California or near a rain forest or the desert? What might biodiversity have to do with the fires in places like Los Angeles? What does it have to do with fish dying of mercury poisoning in our oceans?
>
> I want to know what my students care about and how they are already hooked into this material.

The collage project takes students through a visual journey from accessing their own knowledge, expanding on it, and reflecting on what they have learned and how they can be actively involved in making changes within their community.

A couple of Monica's colleagues also wanted to make their lessons more meaningful to their students' lives. One high school science teacher wanted to get her students involved in a community project such as the local Homeless Garden Project. However, she was daunted by the logistics of researching, making connections, planning, and establishing a protocol for the implementation of such a project. How would the project link to the state science standards? How would students get to and from the garden? What would students do if they couldn't gain their parents' permission to participate? What would they do once they were there? How would they be accountable for their time? How would she build in an assessment component?

Since her school was not a service-learning school, there were no programmatic structures in place to help her with her lesson plan development and implementation. So she too began her biological evolution study with the collage project, adding a research component where each student had to interview a family member about his or her perceptions of how organisms in our world experience interdependency.

Alaina used the collage project in her tenth-grade history class to figure out what her students knew about the Vietnam War. She commented that originally she was looking for a meaningful collaborative activity. We note that the collage activity works well as a joint activity and for contextualizing instruction.

Lesson 3: World History/Geography, Grades 9 and 10

In this lesson, Laura Ianacone Taschek provides an example of how she applied contextualization in her ninth-grade world geography class.

In this unit, Laura examines cultural universals and explores the question "What is culture?" The purpose of the unit is to hypothesize about whether cultural universals exist throughout the world. If so, what are these universal traits, and why do they exist? Laura and her students also examine the assumptions and biases that people hold for different cultures of the world.

Laura describes two activities in which the students build on their own experiences to understand other cultures better. After discussing and analyzing American culture, the students view and collect information from Peter Menzel's *Material World: A Global Family Portrait,*[13] a book that offers photojournalists' views of families from around the world. Students view photos, read interviews, and compare statistics about families from around the globe. They hear personal accounts rather than just read textbook summaries about different cultures and their daily lives. One of Laura's goals is to steer her students away from the "us" and "them" mentality by introducing the universals of "our" cultures.

Lesson: Exploring Culture Activity

Time Estimate: 40 to 60 minutes

Social Science Standards

- Students demonstrate how culture is affected by larger social, economic, political, and historical trends and developments.
- Students analyze how change happens at different rates at different times by exploring essential questions such as Why have certain social, political, and economic elements become international cultural norms? How do values become cultural norms?[14]

Essential Lesson Goals

1. Define the cultural universals that exist throughout the world.
2. Analyze how these elements have come to be universally valued.
3. Become familiar with, examine, and question our assumptions and cultural biases.
4. Consider how we have developed these assumptions.
5. Explore what might be problematic about these assumptions.
6. Provide ways to change our assumptions.

Lesson Plan

1. Students write a journal entry to define culture. For many students, this concept is quite abstract, so ask students to pick a partner and discuss their understandings of culture before they write. Ask them to think about where, when, and how we see our culture in our everyday lives. Say to the students, "With your partner, write any words or images that come to mind when you think of the word *culture*. Try to produce a list of at least ten words."

2. Introduce the template of a culture wheel (similar to a word web) shown in Figure 3.1. Students construct a word wheel to define what they think are attributes of culture. Discuss what types of categories or large ideas could make up a definition of culture.

3. Students in pairs create their own culture word wheel in their journals: "Come up with a key that explains the attributes specific to your own family culture, which items are true of American culture, and which items would represent cultural universals; that is, items that define culture in many different countries" (Figure 3.2).

FIGURE 3.1. CULTURE WHEEL TEMPLATE

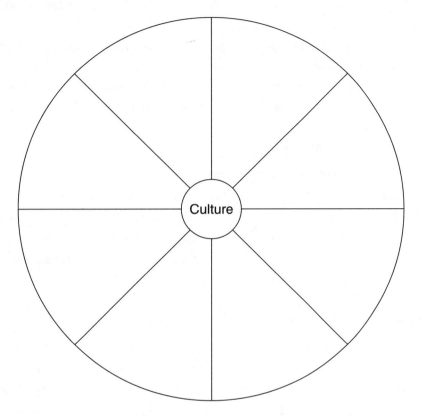

FIGURE 3.2. STUDENT'S CULTURE WHEEL

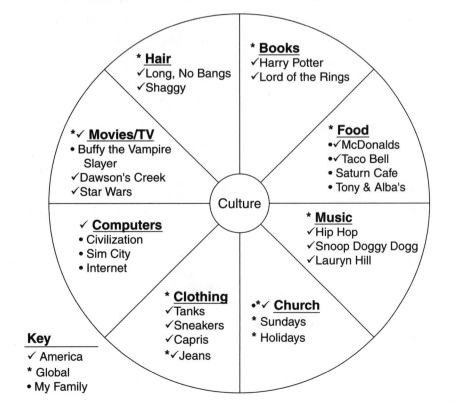

4. After students complete their culture word wheels, pass out the cultural universals diagram in Figure 3.3 and ask them to complete a chart in their journal comparing and contrasting their wheel with this one.

5. Students write a complex, multiparagraph definition and analysis of *culture*. They address the question of how values become cultural norms. They must include at least two examples of how culture is affected by larger social, economic, political, or historical trends and developments. The examples must have supportive research evidence from the Internet or textbooks.

Lesson Assessment

Students are assessed on their culture wheels, written definitions of culture, and analyses of culture. They are informed that they are to look for an evolution in their own thinking. For example, if they began by defining culture as "what we believe in" and concluded the unit with a complex, multiparagraph definition and analysis of culture, then they are working in the A/B letter grade zone. Laura is also looking for personal voice, style, quality of work, and completion.

Commentary on Lesson

Laura comments, "I am always surprised to find that initially, many students define culture with simple phrases such as, 'What you believe in,' 'It's how we live,' 'Culture is what we see on TV," or 'Man, it's the food.'" These students' understanding of culture expand from a simple definition of "what we believe in" to a description of the different attributes of culture. However, there is much room for discussion. Many students believe that religion, books, and movies and TV are universal cultural elements. After this activity, Laura puts students in small groups and has them discuss the universality of these attributes. She asks them to individually write a one-page journal entry explaining the rationale for their thinking.

Students would not initially categorize movies, literature and books, music, and visual art together in the category "Arts." But the diagram in Figure 3.3 helps them think about concepts in a larger way. Many students conclude in their journals that they never quite realized that different cultures all have "arts" but that art is expressed in different forms.

Laura comments, "If students were not encouraged to begin with what they know about their own lives and experiences about culture, this lesson would simply be what it used to be for me: an unfulfilling discussion about some abstract concept called Culture."

FIGURE 3.3. UNIVERSAL CULTURE WHEEL

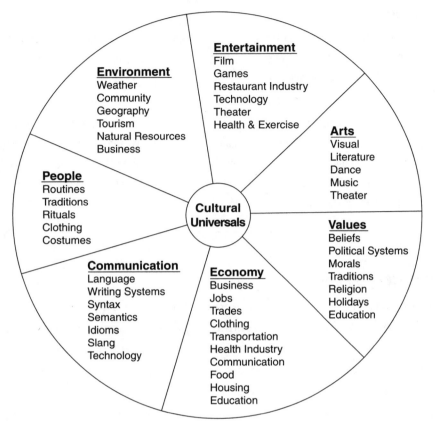

Lesson 4: History/Social Studies, Grade 9 or 10

A second activity that Laura uses to help contextualize the concept of culture is called "Families on the Coastside."

Lesson: Family Interview Project

Time Estimate: One week

Essential Lesson Goals

1. Students explore their own family cultural customs and traditions.
2. By interviewing members of the local community, they compare different family customs and traditions.

Lesson Plan

1. Students use Handout 3.2 to discuss family customs and traditions with their own family members.

2. For homework, students choose one or two community members to interview about culture. They can pick a local shopkeeper, a neighbor, another teacher, someone at their parents' bank, an elderly person in a local nursing home.

3. Students turn in completed interviews.

4. Students are required to complete the unit by doing book and Internet research and writing a report comparing and contrasting two cultures with their own and/or that of a community member. They must address why and how at least two political or economic values have become international cultural norms. How are these values represented through their community interviews as well as through the research?

Commentary on Lesson

Laura has used small-group and whole-group discussion formats to share family stories. This activity was met with such enthusiasm that it prompted her to add the community outreach piece to the unit. Laura and her students worked together to create the community survey, in which they ask for descriptions of family members, cultural heritage, the home environment, a typical day, a typical holiday, a special family activity, the family's most valued possession, and the women in the family and what their typical day is like. The activity helps emphasize the vast diversity of American culture and sets the stage for discussions about and research on other cultures. At the end of the unit, students are required to conduct research and write a report addressing universal cultural values.

The students use their own personal experiences and those of the interviewees to discuss the range of American culture. Recently Laura hosted two guest speakers from Peru and Argentina. After the students researched families from all over the world, they had an opportunity to ask questions about life and culture in Peru and Argentina.

Handout 3.2
Families of the Coastside

Family name:

Country:

Name of family members:

Number of children in family:

Describe the members of your family (ages, genders, characteristics).

(1) Describe a typical weekday with your family.

(2) Describe a typical holiday with your family.

Describe the house your family lives in.

Describe a special family activity (e.g., "Every Sunday is 'Pancake Sunday.'").

Describe the women of the family and what their typical day is like.

What is your family's most valued possession?

Conclusion

In all of the exemplary activities, teachers are making their best effort to design and offer meaningful lessons. The activities capture student interest because they are connected to their lives, whether it is by simulating a historical situation, offering provocative discussions and writing topics, or showing authentic interest in what they know and want to know about a given topic.

At a recent teacher institute day at one of the local schools near San Jose, California, teachers worked together in small groups to create lessons for thematic units. One of our guiding questions was simply "So what?"

- How is the content meaningful to our students?
- What difference will this lesson make to our students' lives?
- How are we integrating community and family knowledge and experiences into the lesson?
- How are students being guided to build on, apply, and expand what they know about a topic?

As we worked throughout the morning, we realized repeatedly that these questions are critical for every learner. However, in order to close the equity gap for English Language Learners, we must consider the relevance of the curriculum and the cultural match or mismatch. For English Language Learners and other students placed at risk, "prior knowledge plays a significant role in learning in terms not only of where to start, but also of the actual meanings attached to the new information." August and Hakuta discovered that English Language Learners perform better in school when traits of learning and talking are similar to those of their homes and communities.[15] This is not to say that we build the curriculum based on only what our students know and are comfortable learning. We use their prior understandings as the starting point in building schemata and expanding their repertoire of knowledge.

Rudolfo Chávez Chávez advocates that "constructing curriculum for achieving equity is an attitude that resonates from a longing to have all students think and do for themselves and others in compassionate ways rooted in respect, dignity, and high expectations."[16] In most of our classrooms, we have a multicultural, often multilingual, population of students. Through getting to know the community, our students, and their families, we orchestrate a classroom community where students' lives and experiences are valued and used as the springboard from which to learn.

Giving students the opportunity to talk about their knowledge as well as apply and expand on their understandings gets to the heart of effective teaching and learning. We want to boost student interest and captivate their motivation with personally relevant and engaging material. We aspire to hear students' voices resonate, "You got me—I finally care!"

Challenging Activities
Teaching Complex Thinking

Good teaching actively involves students in real-life situations, which allows them to reflect on their own lives. . . . Good teaching is taking place when teachers welcome difficult issues and events and use human difference as the basis for the curriculum; design collaborative activities for heterogeneous groups; and help students apply ideals for fairness, equity, and justice to their work.
Ethan Mintz and John T. Yun, *The Complex World of Teaching* (1999)

Mintz and Yun describe the essence of complex thinking. Offering our students challenging activities invites them to broaden their experiences, make connections between divergent ideas, build pathways of knowledge, and develop empathy and compassion for our world and its diversity of people and perspectives. These activities also mean offering students:

- Work that is interesting and provocative
- Work that encourages students to be problem solvers and analysis experts
- Work that forces them to evaluate, synthesize, predict, and design
- Work that supports them to think about their own ideas and thinking

Roland Tharp writes that all students "require instruction that is cognitively challenging, that is, instruction that requires thinking and analysis, not only rote, repetitive, detail-level drills."[1] Although this is true for all students, it is especially true for students placed at risk, specifically when the risk arises from language factors. We often find these students receiving watered-down, drill-based curriculum, instruction, and assessments. Tharp continues:

> At-risk students, particularly those of limited Standard English proficiency, are often forgiven any academic challenges, on the assumption that they are of limited ability; or they are forgiven any genuine assessment of progress, because the assessment tools don't fit. Thus both standards and feedback are weakened, with the predictable result that achievement is handicapped. While such policies may often be the result of benign

motives, the effect is to deny many diverse students the basic requirements of progress: high academic standards and meaningful assessment that allows feedback and responsive assistance.[2]

It is imperative that we offer students a quality educational program that stretches them beyond their current knowledge. While this is important for all students, it is especially important for English Language Learners because of a history of offering insufficient and inappropriate curricula.

The following focus questions provide a guide to implementing the principle of complex thinking. When we teach, we want to make sure that we are appropriately challenging our students to think deeply about the subject matter:

Complex Thinking Focus Questions for Planning Lessons

1. **Consider the type and progression of activities. How do you assist your students in understanding complex tasks or concepts? What scaffolds are you providing? What types of extended activities are offered?**

2. **What type of questions are you asking? How many of your questions require students to provide known, close-ended versus open-ended, higher-order, analytical, and evaluative answers?**

3. **How are you giving students access to your goals, expectations, and assessment/evaluation for their performance/product? Are you modeling the activity? Showing previous, exemplary work? Reviewing a rubric?**

4. **After you present your expectations, how are you giving your students feedback about their work during and after the lesson?[3]**

Disclosing the mandated standards to students and involving them fully and candidly in the assessment process fosters the development of higher-level, complex thinking skills. By involving students, we ask them to *analyze* by comparing and contrasting their work to an established set of criteria such as a rubric. We want them to *evaluate* their work against a standard—either a state standard or an explicitly stated expectation established by the teacher. Finally, we can require them to *synthesize* their work by developing goals and a plan to improve it.

Lessons from the Classroom

Throughout this chapter, teachers use the focus questions as a framework and reflective tool to develop exemplary lessons that implement and highlight the principle of complex thinking. In lesson 1, a pair of teachers take a literature lesson and improve it to incorporate more opportunities for students to engage in challenging activities including self-assessments. In lessons 2 and 3, a social science and a mathematics teacher provide examples of how they enrich their lessons to make them more cognitively demanding. In the final lesson, Laura Ianacone Taschek and her peers create a series of lessons to help students master the process of writing a research paper.

Lesson 1: Literature, Grade 9 or 10

At Forest High School, a small group of high school English teachers explore the principle of complex thinking. Forest High School serves students from several communities. Approximately half of the student population are English Language Learners, ranging from beginning to advanced levels of English language literacy. During initial discussions, this group of four English teachers describes their teaching as "standards based," "necessary for developing English literacy skills," "important for preparing students for college or community college," and "the bare bones of a core understanding of literature." However, they feel that many of their students are not very interested in the material and "are turning in, at best, mediocre work." They want their students to be motivated and interested in reading contemporary works that "deeply reflect on our society's culture and history." They want their students "to be challenged to think, question, debate, argue, and grow in their knowledge and perspectives."

These four teachers take a moment to reflect on the concept of complex thinking using the following questions, which clearly express how teaching higher-order thinking skills relates to their experiences in teaching English Language Learners:

Reflection Questions

1. Describe one learning experience that you've had where you felt challenged in your learning. This experience should be a positive one where you were really able to learn and apply some new skill or concept.

2. Describe one teaching experience where you felt successful in appropriately challenging a student or group of students. Tell about the experience. What happened? Why was this lesson challenging?

3. When you teach, how do you make sure that you are appropriately challenging your students to think deeply about the subject?

This is an excerpt of the conversation that took place among the teachers. The teachers spoke briefly about their own experiences but focused more deeply on how their teaching affects their students:

Marta: As an English Language Learner, I know this firsthand. Offered worksheet after worksheet, the boredom of school. Watching my peers around me getting to read books and have discussions . . . participate in lectures. Teachers always calling on them. And I was only expected to complete these packets of Dittoes. It was tremendously boring, meaningless. It reflects on what Tharp said in his research report, "Handicapped Achievement."[4]

Don: Yes, why would anyone think that just because you don't speak the language, you have limited ability?

Linda: You know, I have been guilty of this. Not now, but when I first began teaching. It was not malicious. It was ignorance. I didn't know what to do with any students who did not fit the normal curriculum—whether they are English Language Learners or challenged because of learning disabilities or attention deficit disorder. It was one-size-fits-all, and if you didn't fit, then read the textbook and answer the questions. It's so true: this type of teaching denies students their basic rights to a fair education, an equitable education.

Chris: I hear this, and I get scared. How am I going to meet all of my students' needs? I always have many different ability levels in one class.

Don: I used to use a lot of lecture. Like all other teachers, I want to give out appropriate and meaningful information without boring or losing my students. However, I realize that I lose them: I bore them, and I lose them. Not all of them, but many, especially the more beginning English Language Learners. Now I use my lectures as an opportunity. I model using visual aids as a scaffold, and I incorporate joint activities such as Kagan's pair share and four square into the lecture so that students have a chance to discuss what I am talking about and how it relates to them.[5]

Marta: From my own experience, I realize that I can't do it alone. Collaborating with other teachers helps me. The collaboration helps me plan instruction and assessments that are more cognitively challenging.

Marta and Linda decide to work as a team to make a lesson from the unit on Maya Angelou more cognitively challenging. In addition to working with curricular and instructional issues, the teachers also start to look at how they include students in the assessment process. They ask, "Do we let our students know the standards that we are teaching? Do we let students know exactly how and why they are being assessed? How do we give them consistent feedback on their progress? What schoolwide systems are in place for giving students feedback? What systems do we have in place in our own classes?"

Their original version of the lesson appears here along with a discussion on how to strengthen the lesson. Then an enhanced version of the lesson follows.

Lesson: *I Know Why the Caged Bird Sings*

Time Estimate: Six to eight days of 60-minute class periods

Lesson Plan

1. Students read *I Know Why the Caged Bird Sings* by Maya Angelou.[6]

2. Students will maintain a journal where they document, in summary form, what happens throughout the book. Each entry needs to describe the main events and should be approximately half a page.

3. After reading the entire book, students will write a five- to eight-page essay on one of the following questions:

    *   "What does the title of this book mean? Why did Maya Angelou choose it, and how does this title reflect the themes of the book?"

    *   "Discuss the most important themes of the book. Describe why these themes are important."

    *   "Pick out at least two adults who influenced Maya Angelou's life. Why were they so important to her? Discuss how these characters helped to build the themes of the book."

Commentary on Lesson

Using the complex thinking focus questions, the teachers focus on ways to increase the complexity of the assignments. In the previous lesson, students are asked merely to summarize the text and then clarify the themes. While theme is an important concept for students to recognize and summarize, Linda and Marta feel that the assignments would be more cognitively challenging by having students analyze the book in greater detail, defend their ideas with supporting textual evidence, and enter their comments into a journal. They also want students to know how they are evaluated. They created a literary analysis rubric (see Exhibit 4.1) that students use as a guide to reflect on their work and how well they complete their assignment. The rubric is versatile in that it can be adapted to evaluate other student work such as a literary journal, essay, research paper, or other writing assignment.

Even more cognitively challenging, Linda and Marta provide students with newspaper articles reporting that several school districts have put a ban on the book. They then ask students to write an editorial discussing whether the book should be banned and explaining their reasoning with supporting evidence from the book. With this assignment, set out in Handout 4.1, students are required to evaluate the book and defend their opinion. The teachers developed a rubric for this task as well (see Exhibit 4.2).

EXHIBIT 4.1. MAYA ANGELOU LITERARY ANALYSIS RUBRIC

4   Exceptional

- Clearly document and explain the plot with details that support the main ideas and themes.
- Thoroughly analyze interactions between main and subordinate characters in the text (for example, internal and external conflicts, motivations, relationships, influences), and explain the way those interactions affect the plot.
- Carefully select quotes as supporting evidence for your opinions and judgments.
- Elaborate on essential perspectives and/or themes.
- Discuss personal insights and reflections. How does the book relate to you?
- Pose thoughtful questions.
- Consistently share excerpts of your journal writing in both small- and large-class discussions to express your point of view.

3   Commendable

- Document and explain the plot with details that support the main ideas and themes.
- Analyze interactions between main and subordinate characters in the text (for example, internal and external conflicts, motivations, relationships, influences), and explain the way those interactions affect the plot.
- Select at least one quote as supporting evidence for your opinions or judgments.
- Document essential perspectives.
- Discuss at least one personal insight or reflection. How does the book relate to you?
- Pose at least one thoughtful question.
- Share excerpts of your journal writing in both small- and large-class discussions to express your point of view.

2   Satisfactory

- Document and explain the plot with details that support the main ideas and themes.
- Analyze interactions between main and subordinate characters in the text (for example, internal and external conflicts, motivations, relationships, influences), and explain the way those interactions affect the plot.
- Need to select at least one quote as supporting evidence for your opinions or judgments.
- Need to discuss at least one personal insight or reflection. How does the book relate to you?
- Occasionally share excerpts of your journal writing in both small- and large-class discussions to express your point of view.

1   Minimal

- Document the plot with minimal details that support the main ideas and themes.
- Need to include an analysis of the interactions between main and subordinate characters in the text (for example, internal and external conflicts, motivations, relationships, influences), and explain the way those interactions affect the plot.
- Need to select at least one quote as supporting evidence for your opinions or judgments.
- Few, if any, personal insights or reflections.
- Minimal, if any, sharing of your journal excerpts in both small- and large-class discussions to express your point of view.

Handout 4.1

Student Assignment for *I Know Why the Caged Bird Sings*

1. You will be reading the text and maintaining a journal where you document, in summary form, what happens throughout the book. Read through the Maya Angelou literary analysis rubric, which requires you to address the themes of the book, analyze the characters, share personal insights, and defend your ideas and perspectives with supporting textual evidence.

2. After reading the entire book, you will be responsible for completing the following assignment. Please research several newspaper articles that discuss how some school districts have banned *I Know Why the Caged Bird Sings*. Take notes on the articles so that you know the authors' points of view and their rationale. Then write an editorial discussing whether the book should in fact be banned from high school reading lists. Explain your reasoning with supporting evidence from the book as well as the articles. With this assignment, you are being required to evaluate the book and defend your opinion. You will be evaluated using the Maya Angelou editorial writing assignment rubric in Exhibit 4.2.[7]

EXHIBIT 4.2. MAYA ANGELOU EDITORIAL WRITING ASSIGNMENT RUBRIC

4 Exceptional
- Gave a comprehensive and accurate interpretation of the evidence, statements, and questions posed in the articles
- Identified, analyzed, and evaluated the most important positive and negative arguments and perspectives
- Thoroughly compared the *time frame* of the articles from the 1980s and 1990s to our present times and analyzed how this work reflects on this historical time period
- Explained your assumptions, evidence, and reasoning
- Drew thoughtful conclusions and judgments about the problems; thoroughly analyzed the complexity of the problems
- Adeptly combined critical thinking, content knowledge, and technical skill to create an exceptional piece of writing

3 Commendable
- Gave an accurate interpretation of the evidence, statements, and questions posed in the articles
- Identified, analyzed, and evaluated relevant positive and negative arguments and perspectives
- Drew some comparisons between the *time frame* of the articles from the 1980s and 1990s to our present times and analyzed how this work reflects on this historical time period
- Explained some of your assumptions, evidence, and reasoning
- Drew conclusions and judgments about the problems; addressed the complexity of the problems
- Combined critical thinking, content knowledge, and technical skill to create a commendable piece of writing

2 Satisfactory
- Gave an interpretation (or possibly some misinterpretation) of the evidence, statements, and questions posed in the articles
- Minimally identified, analyzed, and/or evaluated relevant positive and negative arguments and perspectives
- Drew few, if any, comparisons between the *time frame* of the articles from the 1980s and 1990s to our present times and minimally analyzed how this work reflects on this historical time period
- Needed to explain some of your assumptions, evidence, and reasoning
- Regardless of the evidence, maintained your own interpretations and conclusions based on preconceptions and judgments about the problems; did not address the *complexity* of the problems
- Minimal evidence of critical thinking, content knowledge, or technical skill

1 Minimal
- Obvious misinterpretation of the evidence, statements, and questions posed in the articles
- Did not identify and/or analyze relevant positive and negative arguments and perspectives
- Failed to draw comparisons between the *time frame* of the articles from the 1980s and 1990s to our present times and did not analyze how this work reflects on this historical time period
- Very minimally explained some of your assumptions, evidence, and/or reasoning
- Regardless of the evidence, maintained your own interpretations and conclusions based on preconceptions and judgments about the problems; ignored obvious alternative points of view
- Lacking evidence of critical thinking, content knowledge, or technical skill

Revised Lesson: *I Know Why the Caged Bird Sings*

Time Estimate: Six to eight days of 60-minute class periods

Essential Language Arts Content Standards

- Students analyze interactions between main and subordinate characters in a literary text (for example, internal and external conflicts, motivations, relationship, influences) and explain the way those interactions affect the plot.
- Students engage in literary criticism, analyzing the way in which a work of literature is related to the themes and issues of its historical period.[8]

Learning Objectives

1. Students will analyze the themes of the book and the characters' behaviors, motivations, and feelings.

2. Students will write an editorial defending their position with textual support and references.

3. Students will engage in narrative analysis and literary criticism of the text, meeting the California Language Arts Standards.

Lesson Plan

1. Students will read the text and maintain a journal where they document, in summary form, what happens throughout the book. Students are required to address the themes of the book, analyze the characters, share personal insights, and defend their ideas and perspectives with supporting textual evidence. (Refer to Exhibit 4.1)

2. After reading the entire book, students will be responsible for completing an assignment in which they refute or defend banning the book from high school reading lists.

Commentary on Revised Lesson

The teachers feel that incorporating the rubrics makes a difference in both their teaching and students' learning. At first, they admit they were a little intimidated by having to generate assessments to give to students. Marta reveals, "Right now, I know in my own head what an A looks like, what a B looks like, what a C looks like, what's a D, and what fails. I found it really challenging to spell out my thinking in a rubric form. Once we have the rubric for the students, I can see what a huge difference it makes in the students' work." Marta is elated with the clarity of student work and the writing results: "These papers are some of the best my students have written all year. Laying out the expectations makes a huge difference. We have a common framework to talk about. I don't have to repeat over and over again, 'Where's your supporting evidence? How do you know this? Where is your support?' It is right there spelled out for them. And before they begin writing, I review the editorial rubric and have them highlight the key phrases."

Linda adds that she thinks linking the lesson to the state standards and then incorporating those standards into the rubric helps her feel comfortable about the curriculum she is teaching. "I always worry about pressure from the administration. Am I doing a good job? Am I teaching what the state is asking me to teach? Am I preparing my students for college? By thinking about the Maya Angelou unit and weaving the state standards into the writing rubrics, I feel good—secure that I am doing a good job blending state expectations with what is good for my students. I want my students to be able to comment about how the book is personally meaningful to them. I want them to have an opinion, take a stand."

Both teachers note that in order to make the curriculum meaningful and challenging for their students, they have to stretch their own thinking about the lessons and assignments. Marta comments, "Planning lessons and assessments this way is hard work. Hard work for us! We have to get out our standards and really think about what is appropriate to address in this unit. Creating rubrics is also time-consuming and challenging. . . . We actually took the time to get students' input as well. That helped. Remember Serena and Monty commenting that they thought this will help them know what they are writing about. . . . The good news about this work is now that it's done, it's done! We have something to work with next time we teach the unit."

Linda's final comments summarize her commitment to making changes in the way she designed and taught this lesson:

> I am going to use these new lessons. I believe it will help move students from a superficial understanding of the text to a deeper understanding. We wove in a component that will help them think about how the media affect their own lives. We created what I think is an excellent rubric for assessing their essay. We wove in a place for small-group conversations about their journal writings. And I am excited about having these discussions, especially with my English Language Learners because they rarely talk during our whole-class discussions. I feel that I am offering a more inclusive lesson.

Lesson 2: Social Science, Grades 9 to 11

This social science lesson, developed by Laura Ianacone Taschek, is about global warming. She presents only the original version of the lesson here but uses the focus questions to reflect on the changes she would make to create a more cognitively challenging, rigorous activity.

Lesson: Global Warming Activity

Time Estimate: One 90-minute class

Social Science Standards

- Historical Research, Evidence, and Point of View: Students construct and test hypotheses; collect, evaluate, and employ information from multiple primary and secondary sources; and apply it in oral and written presentations.
- Historical Interpretation: Students analyze environmental policy issues.[9]

Learning Objectives

1. Students write about global warming and what world communities are doing to address the issue.
2. Students identify the positive and negative features of the Kyoto Treaty.

Lesson Plan

1. Briefly discuss the historical research and salient features of global warming. Highlight the Kyoto Summit meeting and treaty.
2. Students read one of the following articles about global warming from the perspective of its being a global environmental policy issue:
   - M. Lemonick, "Hot Air in Kyoto," *Time,* December 8, 1997, pp. 79–80.
   - J.F.O. McAllister, "Forecast: Heat Wave," *Time,* October 13, 1997, p. 36.
3. Students pick a partner and read the following two articles:
   - National Environmental Trust, "Developing Countries and Climate Change: The Kyoto Treaty Is Fair and It Will Work" (May 1998), http://www.envirotrust.com/fairtreaty.html.
   - World Wildlife Fund, "Kyoto Conference Report" (May 1998), http://www.panda.org/climate/kyoto/report.html.

   Together the partners create a chart that contrasts the two different perspectives of the articles.
4. Students conduct Web-based research and write a brief report about what they learned. (Refer to Handout 4.2 for student instructions.)

Conduct of Lesson

Laura presents a brief mini-lecture that includes significant vocabulary from the articles. Then she passes out Handout 4.2. Amid a couple of comments such as, "Oh, my mom is always talking about this," "So much work for us, Ms. Taschek!" and "We had an exchange student from Kyoto a couple of years ago," students begin selecting their initial article to read. Following this, they quickly choose a partner, begin to read a second set of articles, and discuss the attributes of their chart.

Handout 4.2
Student Assignment for
"Our Environment: Global Warming"

For the past ten years, many scientists have argued about whether global warming is a reality. Today scientists have mostly agreed that global warming is a problem, and something needs to be done about it. In December 1997, 170 nations met in Kyoto, Japan, to discuss a world solution to the global warming problem. The meeting produced a controversial treaty that a majority of the countries of the world signed. In this assignment, you will read about the controversy that plagued the Kyoto Summit meeting and the treaty that was signed. You will get to decide for yourself whether the treaty is a good thing.

1. Read one of these two articles: "Hot Air in Kyoto," which discusses the importance of and need for a successful summit, or "Forecast: Heat Wave," which explores what policy decisions the United States will make about global warming.

2. One of the biggest concerns during the summit was whether developing nations were doing their share to reduce their greenhouse gases, such as CO_2 (carbon dioxide) emissions. Most major sources of greenhouse gases come from the burning of fossil fuels (gas, oil, and coal), forest destruction, and agriculture. Choose one of the following activities to complete:

   • The remaining two handouts provide a discussion about the Kyoto Treaty. One article, "The Kyoto Treaty Is Fair and It Will Work," supports the Kyoto Treaty, and the other, "Kyoto Conference Report," identifies some flaws in the treaty. Create a chart that lists the arguments for and against the treaty. Use what you learn from these articles to fill in the chart.

   • Sign out at the front desk to visit the library or computer lab. Browse through one or all of the Web sites listed below; spend about fifteen minutes looking at the site. After you finish, write a one-page response about what you learned and what questions you still have about global warming.

   http://www.epa.gov/globalwarming

   http://www.globalwarming.org/

   http://www.sierraclub.org/globalwarming/

   http://www.envirotrust.com

Commentary on Lesson

Laura reflects on the lesson using the complex thinking focus questions. She feels successful about requiring students to create products that are challenging and require higher-level thinking skills: "I like the comparison chart. I think this type of analysis is good for students. They have to think about the reading, take it apart, and look at the different ideas and perspectives." Because students are being required to produce the chart, they use and apply some of the vocabulary, such as *global warming, Kyoto Treaty, greenhouse effect, carbon-based fuels,* and *emissions target.* The students are required to create a product that is difficult: comparing and contrasting, reading and synthesizing information. Also, the students review and compare information from several sources.

There are four areas that Laura feels she wants to improve. The first area is assessment. She recognizes that she does not provide students a way of knowing her expectations. There is no modeling, previous exemplary work for students to compare, rubric, or other guideline delineating the expectations. For example, how many points do they need to address in the chart? What needs to be included in their one-page response? How will they be graded on their work? How will they get feedback about their work?

The second area Laura wants to improve is connecting the lesson to students' knowledge base and experiences. She suggests, "Maybe I'll have students address a question like, 'How does this information affect our daily life?' or 'What impact does global warming have on us in our day-to-day existence?' I want them to care about global warming and not just see it as another topic to be covered in class."

Third, Laura thinks that she could have increased the cognitive complexity of the task by having students take a position and defend their opinion, drawing on the readings for evidence and support. She also considers requiring them to draw conclusions from the information they read.

Finally, Laura comments that the lesson would be improved if the essential ideas or questions are laid out at the beginning of the task. She decided to add this to the beginning of the task: "Global Warming: Is it a reality or a myth? How are different countries addressing the problem?" Then all the reading and research would be focused around answering these questions.

Lesson 3: Trigonometry, Grade 11

After a few years of teaching, William aspires to modify his math instruction to include more student engagement. He wants his students to be challenged to engage with the material not only by listening to lectures and completing a series of problems and exams, but by talking about the ideas, explaining the concepts to each other, and comparing their performance to his expectations as well as their own expectations. His instruction illustrates a conventional math lesson. Using the focus questions, he discusses how to make improvements and offers an enriched lesson.

Lesson: Trigonometry

Time Estimate: One or two 53-minute class periods

Essential Mathematics Standards

1. Review the applications and word problems of trigonometry.

2. Introduce students to salient vocabulary and introductory concepts: Determine unknown sides or angles in right triangles; know the law of sines and the law of cosines; apply those laws to solve problems.[10]

Lesson Plan

1. Lecture: Talk with students about where and why we use trigonometry.
   - Explain how the trigonometric tables were created over two thousand years ago. They were originally created for astronomical calculations.
   - Discuss the difference between plane and spherical trigonometry; how spherical trigonometry has been replaced by linear algebra.
   - Reference Ptolemy and Columbus's use of trigonometry.
   - Explain the movement from spheres to planes (greater application).

2. Demonstrate on the board a triangle with a right (90-degree) angle. Label the sides.

3. Explain definitions of *sine, cosine, tangent, adjacent angle,* and *hypotenuse.* Determine unknown sides or angles of right triangles; sines and cosines; work with unknowns when determining the area of a triangle.

4. Demonstrate how to use a calculator to determine the arctangent.

5. Have students complete introductory problems in the text while I rotate around room answering questions and checking work.

Commentary on Lesson

William recognizes that he has clear goals, guided by the state mathematics standards. He also realizes that he is an expert at modeling and demonstrating how to complete problems. He is adept at talking aloud the process he uses to solve both simple and complex problems. He comments, "For me, it is very challenging to look at my math lesson and rethink how I would teach it to make it more cognitively complex. I am writing lessons quickly because I have so many lessons to do. So I have developed some bad habits of requiring the bare minimum. I have the students do a lot of problems out of the textbook and then take the end-of-unit test."

William aspires to improve the ways he teaches the lesson and involve students in his lectures. Using the focus questions as a framework, he thinks about how to get students to think more deeply about mathematical ideas. His ideas focus on four areas:

- **Communicate goals, expectations, and assessments protocols.** He comments, "I always know what I am working toward, and I think it would help to tell students as well what we are learning and why. I can put the standards and objectives in the PowerPoint presentation."

- **Provide more of a conceptual foundation about the topic.** Rather than just starting into the lecture about the trigonometric tables being created two thousand years ago, he wonders if it would be helpful to give students the overarching framework of trigonometry. He ponders, "Maybe put the lecture on PowerPoint. Start out with a simple definition of trigonometry—the study of angles. It's a continuation of geometry, but it allows us to work with angles in more complex ways—like figure out the angle of a cue ball in a pool game or the angle of a soccer ball. It is also critical in the study of astronomy as well as navigation. I think it would also be helpful to brainstorm with students about how trigonometry is relevant and applicable to our lives."

He considers having students read short articles about trigonometry. Working in pairs, each person reads a different excerpt and then shares the information with his or her partner. Then each writes a summary of what he or she learned about trigonometry from reading the articles. This activity provides another way of helping students access the history and concepts about trigonometry.

- **Involve students in pair shares.** "I assess students on the textbook problems and exams. Things for me to think about are how I differentiate instruction. I always have a couple of students who bomb out on solving problems and the exams. I am always wondering how I can work with them." William hopes that by pausing his lectures and pairing students to solve problems, students who are lost will get a little extra support from a peer who can explain the concept. He can discuss a single triangle, model how to label it, and explain the vocabulary. After this explanation, he could pause and ask students to take five minutes to quiz each other about the vocabulary and definitions. They can ask each other: "What is sine? What is cosine? How do we figure out the degrees of the right angle?" Following the calculator demonstration, once again William could pause and ask students to practice doing calculations with a partner.

- **Provide extensions.** Problems in trigonometry are complex and extremely challenging. Students are working with higher mathematical operations. The problems are multistep and require holding several pieces of information simultaneously. To make the work more relevant, William did some research and discovered the useful *Math Forum* Web site, where real-life, complex problems are presented.[11] The problems require higher-order, analytical, and evaluative thinking. Students can solve the problem in different ways. The problems are always interesting and challenging. One *Trigonometry Problem of the Week* had students figuring out the regularity or irregularity of a professional soccer field. Students can work on a problem like this individually or, better, with a partner or two. These challenging problems encourage students to use higher-level thinking skills.

Lesson 4: Writing Research Papers, Grades 9 to 12

In this research section, Laura Ianacone Taschek took the principle of complex thinking, and then designed and implemented a series of lessons in collaboration with her fellow ninth-grade English and social sciences teachers about the process of writing a research paper. They created a series of lessons that assist students in developing appropriate research questions, understanding closed versus open-ended questions, reflecting on the research process, and writing a research paper. Although the assignment requires students to read and think about Tibet, this lesson can be applied to any research topic.

Laura and the other teachers work within a block scheduling system; they have a ninety-minute class period. Their goal was to teach students about the process of writing a research paper. Their motivation was to prepare students for the research papers that they were yet to write in their years of high school and beyond.

Most of us remember at some time in our schooling the experience of taking a topic, such as mountain climbing, and searching the library card catalogue or a search engine on the Internet. Suddenly we find ourselves with a stack of books or a list of over a thousand Web sites. How does one manage this much information? For this reason, teaching students to write appropriate questions to help guide their research is enormously important.

One unique aspect of this assignment is that the students are allowed to choose their topic within parameters set by books they read in their English class. Students brainstorm ideas and topics brought up by the books' themes. Each class produces a large butcher-paper list that hangs in the halls to help students choose their topics. Once the students have chosen their topic, Laura teaches them how to come up with the important, essential questions that will guide their research.

Lesson: Writing Research Papers

Time Estimate: Approximately one to two weeks of 90-minute class periods

Standard (Literature and Social Science)

- Students conduct research on issues and interests by generating ideas and questions and by posing problems. They gather, evaluate, and synthesize data from a variety of sources to communicate their discoveries in ways that suit their purpose and audience.[12]

Learning Objectives

1. Students will ask pertinent and relevant research questions.
2. Students will research (gather, evaluate, and synthesize) a topic using multiple sources.
3. Students will reflect on and document the process of writing a research paper.
4. Students will draft (using an outline format) and write a research paper.

Lesson Plan for Writing Appropriate Research Questions (One to Two Periods)

1. Say, "So, you know what you want to write about. Now what? Whether you are writing about a self-chosen topic or researching the history of Watergate (What's that?), you need research questions to guide your work. In this unit, I model how to come up with effective research questions. It's also okay to change your questions if they don't work; it is all part of the learning process."

2. Introduce students to closed versus open-ended questions by leading them through a "dating game" activity. Ask them to write down three questions they would ask a potential girlfriend or boyfriend. (Students will need to have a journal or notebook for this research assignment.)

3. Invite students to share their questions with the class. Organize the list of questions on the board into two categories: Closed and Open-Ended. Here is how some responses have been grouped:

Closed or Dead-End Questions	*Open-Ended Questions*
Where is your favorite place to eat?	What was your childhood like?
Do you like to ski?	What is your ideal girlfriend or boyfriend?
What is your favorite music group?	Give me three reasons that you want to go
Do you have a cell phone?	out on a date with me.

4. Ask students to differentiate between the two columns. Initiate a discussion about different types of questions. Closed or dead-end questions require only a one-word response: "no" or "yeah," or "my own kitchen." Open-ended questions require sharing and discussion.

5. Tie question-writing skills to the research topic. Discuss: "What type of questions should we ask about our topic? Why is it important to ask these kinds of questions?" Explain that it is important that research questions be open-ended so that the subject can be explored and examined from a multitude of perspectives.

6. Provide students with a background article about the history and present times of Tibet [or other topic], and ask them to skim it briefly.

7. Brainstorm a list of questions—open-ended research questions—that students can address in order to write a paper about Tibet. You may first need to ask the "5 W" questions: Who, What, Where, When, and Why. These "literal questions" serve as a springboard for discussing the foundational facts of a topic. For an example of a graphic organizer the students created as a group, see Appendix 3.

8. Ask the class to choose the best questions and record them on the board.

9. After modeling effective, open-ended research questions, ask students to write up four or five research questions for their chosen research topics as homework.

10. On day 2, have students share their questions in small groups. Give them editorial license to suggest changes to questions in order to improve them.

11. Rejoin as a whole group and do a call-out: each student reads aloud to the class the question he or she likes the best. Suggest minor changes to questions that need editing.

Lesson Plan for Research (One to Three Periods)

1. Encourage students to start their research by answering one of their questions. Their job is to find as much information about that one question and take notes on it. They may be given one or two days to complete this process.

2. After each research day, require students to reflect on the process in their research journals by writing a brief paragraph on each research reflection question:

    *   **What did you do with your research time?**
    *   **What discoveries did you make about your topic?**
    *   **What ideas surprised you? Why?**
    *   **What ideas do you want to know more about?**
    *   **How will you spend your time tomorrow?**

Lesson Plan for Generating Research Paragraphs

1. Both the original four or five questions that guide students' research and the reflection questions become part of the final paper. The reflection paragraphs serve to assist students in interpreting and analyzing their research findings.

2. Assessment (writing research papers): Before the students start their final paper, explain the assessment process to students and introduce the rubric shown in Table 4.1. The rubric assists students in knowing the expectations of the assignment. It can also help them craft interesting questions.[13]

Commentary on Lesson

As Laura works through the steps of this unit, she is with her students every step of the way. She laughs with them as they play the "dating game." Students become enthusiastic about discussing good questions to ask on dates. There is lively conversation and many chuckles. The topic draws them in so that even when the subject changes to discussing possible research questions about Tibet, there is much student participation:

Teacher: Okay, if you were doing a research paper on Tibet, what would you like to know?

Student 1: When were they in power, and when did the Chinese government come to power?

Student 2: What is the religion of the people of Tibet?

Teacher: Yes, that would be good information to know. Should we put that on the chart?

Student 3: No, those questions won't work.

Teacher: Why not?

TABLE 4.1. RESEARCH PAPER RUBRIC

	4—Proficient (Mastering)	3—Developing	2—Emerging (Beginning)
Research Questions: What is important for me to know?	The research questions are described clearly, completely, and in great detail.	The research questions are described, but some details are missing.	The research questions are incompletely and inadequately described.
Findings Paragraphs: What important information did I find out?	The findings paragraphs are described completely and in great detail. Newly learned vocabulary and concepts are integrated. There is an exemplary diversity of (books, magazines, journals, Internet resources) and quantity of research materials. The information collected comprehensively and thoroughly answers the questions.	The findings paragraphs are described adequately with minimal detail. Newly learned vocabulary and concepts are occasionally integrated. There is a minimal diversity (books, magazines, journals, Internet resources) and quantity of research materials. The information collected answers the questions.	The findings paragraphs are described inadequately with minimal detail. Newly learned vocabulary and concepts are not integrated. There is a lack of diversity (books, magazines, journals, Internet resources) and quantity of research materials. The information collected inadequately answers the questions.
Research Reflection Paragraphs: How do I analyze and interpret the information I discovered?	The reflection paragraphs provide a thorough and thoughtful discussion of the research process. They reveal patterns, concepts, or structures in the information. In addition, comparisons, interpretations, inferences, and/or deductions are made. The information is personally relevant. New, sophisticated ideas are presented; suggestions for improving the current situation or problem are identified; and/or recommendations for social action are made.	The reflection paragraphs provide an adequate discussion of the research process. They reveal at least one pattern, concept, or structure in the information. In addition, some comparisons, interpretations, inferences, and/or deductions are made. The information is personally relevant. One new idea is presented; and/or one suggestion for improving the current situation or problem is identified; and/or one recommendation for social action is made.	The reflection paragraphs provide a minimal discussion of the research process. They reveal neither patterns, concepts, or structures in the information nor comparisons, interpretations, or deductions. There is a lack of personal relevance in the discussion in that no new ideas or suggestions made that address the situation or problem.
Conventions	Accurate and consistent standard writing conventions, including grammar, usage, punctuation, capitalization, and spelling. Accurate use of writing conventions as well as organizational structure and presentation consistently enhance the readability of paper.	Developing use of standard writing conventions including grammar, usage, punctuation, capitalization, and spelling. Most of the time, accurate use of writing conventions as well as organizational structure and presentation.	Need to demonstrate use of standard writing conventions including grammar, usage, punctuation, capitalization, and spelling. Errors may distract your paper and make it difficult to read. Needs extensive editing and organizing.

Student 3: They are closed.

Teacher: How do we know they are closed?

Student 4: There is only one answer to those questions. When did they come to power? The answer will be a date, and that is it.

Teacher: Okay, good. So, can anyone think of another way to ask those questions?

Student 5: How about, "What do the people of Tibet believe in? And how does that affect their daily lives?"

Teacher: Good, can we also add, "What is the basis of their belief system?"

Student 5: Yeah, that sounds good.

Student 6: Couldn't we also say: "What is the history of Tibet?" That would talk about what they believe in.

Teacher: Yes, good—that works, too. I think either question would be good. We'll write them both down.

Laura also shares their frustration as they struggle to create meaningful, interesting, open-ended questions. Students brainstorm the following examples:

- What is the basis of their belief system? Or what is the history of Tibet?
- What is the relationship between Tibet and China? What is their history?
- What is Tibet's policy toward women's rights?
- What is daily life like for the people of Tibet?

And she walks around the class, providing feedback and assistance to students as they help each other edit their questions.

One of the main goals of this lesson is to have students recognize the complexity of writing a research paper. It takes organizational skills. It demands higher-level thinking to sort out the details from the important ideas and concepts. It requires students to view a topic from many perspectives: historical, political, religious, cultural, racial, and socioeconomic. Finally, it necessitates self-discipline and motivation to establish a time line and meet daily goals. Laura comments, "The process can be so daunting. One way we have students think about the writing and research process is through the meta-cognitive questioning. It gives them a chance to pause and really consider what they are learning, what is exciting, and what questions they have."

Laura recognizes the commitment she and her colleagues have made to providing students with cognitively challenging activities: "We want to push them past acquiring the minimum standards. We want them to be challenged, motivated, and inspired by the academic work and expectations. We want the curriculum to be complex and meaningful in addition to having personal relevance for our students. As educators, we recognize that we are challenging ourselves to think differently about school and learning."

Conclusion

Teaching complex thinking in our classrooms requires us to become part of the learning process. As high school teachers, we are subject matter experts. We know both national and international history; our understandings of mathematical concepts are vast and deep; we have read and analyzed the themes of *In the Time of Butterflies* by Julia Alvarez twenty-five times.[14] Teaching in this manner requires us to unpack our own thinking. We have internalized our knowledge and do not always realize how much we understand that our students have yet to learn. Encouraging students to grow cognitively demands that teachers challenge, assess, and assist themselves in the learning process. Our perceptions of the effort involved in designing and teaching cognitively challenging learning activities often discourage us from trying it. This is the level of work that makes classroom teaching exciting, challenging, and meaningful to both us and our students.[15]

Teaching Through Dialogue
The Instructional Conversation

These quotations reflect our need to be active participants—co-constructors—in our own learning. How many times have we heard a colleague say, "I really didn't know this material myself, and then I had to teach it. Boy, you really learn something when you have to teach it to someone else."

Teaching through dialogue or conversation has transformative potential. Consider the scenario in which you walk out of a movie theater with friends, completely perplexed by the characters or story line. For many people, the first question is, "How did you like the movie?" After this first question, a conversation ensues in which your friends explain their interpretation and you contribute yours. From this conversation, your initial understandings transform. You are able to gain a more complex and meaningful perspective on the film. You learn with your friends what you could not have constructed on your own.

Instruction through dialogue has been referred to as classroom discourse, Socratic teaching, and small-group discussions. Tharp and Gallimore refer to it as the *instructional conversation* because the conversation must be instructional in intent. The conversation revolves around a piece of text or academic experience. The discourse must have a clearly defined goal. The teacher must be present to assess the students' understandings about the topic and assist them to the next level of learning.[1]

Simultaneously, the instruction must be conversational in the sense that the teacher connects the students' contributions to the essential idea. In an article on instructional conversations, Goldenberg states, "It might appear as an excellent discussion conducted by a teacher and a group of students. It is interesting and engaging; about an idea or concept that has meaning and relevance for students."[2] Through the conversation, students reveal their knowledge and culture, perceptions and beliefs.

The process of assisting a student in moving from one level of learning to the next, higher level is referred to as *working within an individual student's zone of proximal development* (ZPD). Originally defined by Lev Vygotsky, the ZPD describes a continuum of learning: "Initially all learning requires the assistance of a more capable other such as a parent, teacher, expert, or peer. In the second stage of learning, assistance is provided by the self through self-talk. This self-talk can be documented as a verbal process or a silent process that simply occurs on the mental plane of the learner. Finally, the self-talk becomes truncated and the new skill, ability, or concept becomes internalized. In the fourth stage, 'de-automatization' or 'recursion' can occur due to the input of new information, forgetfulness, stress, environmental change, or trauma. The learner can restore their knowledge by using self-talk, or in some instances, relying on the assistance of a more expert other."[3]

The instructional conversation is a powerful teaching tool when applied correctly. It allows students to share and develop their ideas, connect their own experiences, activate prior knowledge, develop new concepts, and apply new language and vocabulary through the means of the discussion.

An instructional conversation must be meaningful and focus on the communication of content matter. It is not best used as a drill-and-practice session of grammatical rules or recitation session of chemical elements. These skills require "right" or "correct" responses. The instructional conversation is used in all content areas—science, mathematics, technology, history, and literature—to promote higher-level thinking skills. It requires students to engage in analysis, synthesis, and evaluation. At the same time, they must develop mastery over language forms and functions (syntax and semantics) to manipulate the ideas in a meaningful way.

The Teacher's Role

The teacher plays a pivotal role in the discussion. It is the teacher who establishes the goals, assesses the comprehension of material, and assists students to the next, or higher, level of knowledge. We truly want students to walk away from the conversation thinking about the material more deeply or from a new perspective.

The teacher sets the structure of the conversation as well: uniting students' personal experiences and previous understandings to the academic concepts. Teachers are present to be subject matter experts, clarify misunderstandings, ask meaningful and appropriately challenging questions, model how to participate effectively in a conversation, offer opinions if necessary, provide examples, elicit the "Aha!" and assist students to engage in meta-cognitive thinking, communicating how they are thinking about particular ideas.

Planning Lessons with Instructional Conversations

The focus questions for this chapter provide a template for teachers to analyze and reflect on their instructional conversations.[4] *One of the most important and powerful factors of the instructional conversation is that all five of the instructional principles outlined in this book exist within it simultaneously.* The conversation supports the teaching of complex language and content goals. It is contextualized within the students' experiences and prior knowledge base. Students model for each other the meta-cognitive process of thinking about specific subject matter. Several students have recounted, "The conversation takes you places that you could never go alone." Finally, the instructional conversation is an effective joint activity with a clear goal and product.

Instructional Conversation Focus Questions

1. **What do you want students to learn from the conversation that they did not know before participating in it? How are you blending language and content learning?** *(Clearly articulated instructional language and content goals)*

2. **How are you linking the conversation to a piece of educational text or an academic experience? How are you requiring the students to support their views and rationales with text evidence?** (*Scaffolding instruction:* **text, pictures, charts, or models, for example**)

3. **What are the open-ended questions that will help guide the conversation?** *(Complex thinking)*

4. **What tangible (a chart) or intangible (drawing a conclusion) product will you create together?** *(Joint productive activity)*[5]

5. **How are you going to ensure that all students are included in the conversation?** *(Inclusion and equity of participation)*

6. **How are you planning on finding out and integrating the students' views, judgments, rationales, and experiences into the conversation?** *(Contextualized instruction)*

7. **How are you assessing your students' talk and thinking process during the conversation?** *(Assessment)*

Benefits of the Instructional Conversation

A growing body of research illuminates the effectiveness of the instructional conversation. In particular studies, students' reading comprehension scores went up with the consistent use of instructional conversations. This rise in scores was true for all students, and especially for English Language Learners.[6] This type of dialogic teaching engages students as active participants. It benefits all students, especially English Learners and other students who might be reticent to participate in a whole-group discussion.

Through the use of instructional conversations, students can become teachers, and teachers can become learners. Each participant in the conversation shares thoughts and knowledge. Collectively, participants build on each other's ideas, constructing meaning out of material that once may have seemed incomprehensible. The instructional conversation is a way of teaching and learning through dialogue.

Structuring the Instructional Conversation

One of the most frequent concerns that arise around using the instructional conversation is its structure. Teachers fear that simply having a conversation with their students about a particular subject will turn into a therapeutic counseling session; degenerate into a chaotic, aimless bantering of ideas; or, worse yet, be reduced to a high school gossip session. I stress the importance of setting a clear instructional goal and maintaining a high level of organization. Teachers can establish a standards-based content goal and a language goal if it is appropriate to the lesson. Examples of language goals include teaching students how to write an effective paragraph, using specific content-related vocabulary in their writing, and working on editing skills.

Although the organizational structure can vary, the sequence in Exhibit 5.1 works effectively for both teachers and students. I expect students to read the material that we will be discussing ahead of time. It is important to remember that it is the text, a scientific experiment, or a specific academic experience relating to explicit content matter that always serves as the foundation for the instructional conversation.

Organizing Conversational Activities

There are three major ways of organizing instructional conversation activities.[7] In the first way, teachers can facilitate an instructional conversation among the whole group of students. We can practice the skills involved in being an effective facilitator:

- Design and ask open-ended, higher-level thinking questions
- Practice reducing teacher talk time and increasing student participation
- Develop joint products together, such as a word web or other graphic organizers

Although holding instructional conversations among the whole class is managerially efficient and allows time for the teacher to practice facilitation skills, it is not as

---

EXHIBIT 5.1. INSTRUCTIONAL CONVERSATION SEQUENCE

1. **Connection questions:** Ask students to describe or explain some event or experience in their own life that relates to the subject matter. Teachers ask questions such as "How have you experienced this situation or a situation similar to this? What do you already know about this subject? When have you experienced this phenomenon? What happened? Where were you? What did you do? Evaluate how the people around you responded."

2. **Weaving questions:**[a] Ask students to think about how their own experience or knowledge relates to the material. Teachers ask, "How does your experience compare to what happens in the text? How did you and the main character respond in a similar manner? How did you respond differently? Judge whether you or the character had a better response to the situation. Why do you think this is so? Building off what you already know, let's begin to discuss a design for a product that illustrates the concepts [of the given subject matter]."

3. **Text support:** Ask students to provide supporting evidence for their ideas with references from the text. Teachers ask, "How do you know this is true? Where did you get that idea? How did you infer that conclusion from the text? How did you solve that problem? What supports your solution from the text?"

4. **Joint production/conclusion:** The students and teacher create a product together. The product can be intangible, such as drawing a conclusion or verbally summarizing the discussion. The product can also be tangible, such as documenting the information in chart form, completing a collaborative lab report, or creating a word web.

5. **Follow-up seatwork/homework:** Always send the students away with some follow-up work to the discussion. Examples include having students answer a few reflection questions about the conversation, compose a brief essay about what they learned, write up a report documenting a solution to a given problem, formulate a hypothesis, develop a design, or predict an outcome.

[a] The term *weaving* is used in Tharp, R. G., & Gallimore, R. (1988). *Rousing minds to life: Teaching, learning, and schooling in social context.* Cambridge: Cambridge University Press. I gave the teachers excerpts of this book to read, and they thought the term was appropriate to describe the task of blending students' prior knowledge with new material.

---

desirable for students because it is impossible for each student to participate in the conversation. It is not possible to get equity of participation. There are always students who will not talk or talk only minimally in a whole-group setting. Although these students benefit from observing the dialogue of their peers, there is limited opportunity for them to develop their verbal skills and expression.

In the second way, teachers can have brief conversations with students in an ad hoc manner. Teachers can float from group to group, offering short instructional conversations to small groups. This method makes the conversation responsive to the issues students are addressing, but it does not permit the teacher to plan an in-depth discussion of major topics or texts.

Finally, the most desirable way to have instructional conversations is on a regular basis with small groups of students. Students then have the opportunity to participate in in-depth conversations using academic concepts and vocabulary. Instructional conversations promote equity within the classroom setting because all students are expected and encouraged to participate. Teachers must check themselves carefully to make sure their own talk time does not exceed student talk time. In fact, students should carry the weight of the conversation, with the teacher functioning as a questioner and clarifier. The teacher also serves as a facilitator, making sure that the conversation is not dominated by one or two verbally proficient students. The teacher purposefully questions, challenges, encourages, or remains quiet, providing instruction, elaboration, and clarification when needed.

Time Management

Depending on how long the class period is, some teachers structure one or two days of the week for instructional conversations. During this time, they either have students work on independent projects or run a series of learning centers on a specific topic. This allows time for the teacher to hold instructional conversations with small groups of students. Depending on how the teacher wants to manage the class, she or he can meet with one group every class period or with several groups. Table 5.1 shows one teacher's schedule. This school operates with a block scheduling system, so class periods are ninety minutes long. Teachers with shorter class periods can structure instructional conversations within their time block. With this schedule, the teacher is able to meet with four groups of seven or eight students each for an instructional conversation one day per week. Each instructional conversation is approximately thirty minutes.

Encouraging Student Participation

In order to have an interesting and thoughtful instructional conversation that is a learning experience, the participants need to have effective listening skills. Learning how to participate in a conversation as a considerate listener and a thoughtful contributor takes time and training. Teachers can develop mini-lessons on these subjects, elucidating the characteristics of good listeners and effective participants. It is interesting to note that we high school teachers take it for granted that our students will come to us with these skills accomplished. Small-group conversational etiquette includes the ability to listen to other students' contributions, make additional comments that enhance or expand on their ideas, ask thoughtful questions about the subject at hand, contribute when there is an appropriate opening in the conversation so as not to talk over someone else, develop an awareness of when one is talking too long or too much—dominating the conversation or not contributing to the flow and development of ideas. Learning to become an effective conversationalist is a lifelong skill and practice.

Instructional conversations are highly beneficial to English Language Learners. They provide a context in which to practice using English in meaningful ways. However, the teacher must provide these learners with vocabulary as well as visual and conceptual support. Use scaffolds such as demonstrating the product, writing down important concepts and vocabulary, and using any visual aids that will support the learners in understanding the ideas.

TABLE 5.1. SCHEDULE FOR CLASSROOM CONVERSATION

Times	Monday	Tuesday	Wednesday	Thursday	Friday
7:40–7:50	Review agenda and any business	Review agenda and any business	Review agenda and any business	Review agenda and any business	Review agenda and any business
7:50–8:20	Mini-lecture and notes	Mini-lecture and notes	Independent seatwork/project and instructional conversation	Independent seatwork/project and instructional conversation	Mini-lecture and notes
8:50–9:15	Discussions and questions	Discussions and questions	Independent seatwork/project and instructional conversation	Independent seatwork/project and instructional conversation	Discussions and questions

Teachers can use participation structure cards as a tool to help students learn the structure of a conversation.[8] The cards provide a specific framework to help students learn how to take turns and share their ideas in a small-group setting. The cards are best used only with upper elementary and middle school students. There are only four roles, set out in the participation structure cards in Exhibit 5.2. Since a teacher will have more than four students participating in an instructional conversation, not everyone will have a card. Some students will be only participants in the conversation.

The teacher can pass these cards out to different students in the group. The student who has card 1 would first ask classmates if they are prepared for the discussion. Do they have their materials and something to write with? After this, the teacher shares her goals with the group. For example, in Lesson 1: Forensic Science, which follows, Sarah, the teacher, could explain that she wants students to (1) compare and contrast the processes of preservation and (2) evaluate the impact of cryonics on our culture. Then she would ask a connection question, followed by a weaving question that requires text support. After this, she would request that the student with card 2 ask for a volunteer to continue the conversation: "Who would like to share an idea?" The student with card 3 keeps the conversation going by asking someone else to make a comment or ask a question about the previous idea: "Who has a question or comment about this idea?"

If students are reluctant to speak, ask the card holders to call on the students in the group. Finally, the student with card 4 leads the group in a reflection activity: "How did this instructional conversation go, and what could we do to improve it next time?"

These cards work well in distributing the talk time evenly in the group. They help students learn how to hold a conversation. However, they serve only as a scaffold; they

---

EXHIBIT 5.2. PARTICIPATION STRUCTURE CARDS

Card 1	**Card 2**
Is everyone prepared for the instructional conversation? Please make sure you have the following items: [List what everyone needs to have with them.]	Who would like to share an idea? (You are in charge of making sure everyone gets a chance to talk.)

Card 3	**Card 4**
Who has a question or comment about this idea?	How did this instructional conversation go today? What can we do to improve it next time?

---

are not intended to be used throughout the entire year. The teacher's goal is to have students learn to make meaningful contributions and be effective listeners within the conversation structure itself.

Differentiated Instruction

To accommodate the range of students we teach, we must offer a diversity of materials and range of reading levels. The teachers in the lessons in this chapter searched for a variety of articles ranging from a fifth- through a twelfth-grade reading level. Having low literacy skills can be embarrassing to students. If we can provide articles, Web sites, or CDs that cross a broad spectrum of reading levels, students can access the text or information at their level. We can provide information through videotapes and audiotapes. We can also work out arrangements so that specific students work with a peer who is able to read the material aloud or in collaboration with them.

There are many ways to work with students who do not read the material ahead of time depending on the student, his or her abilities, and how this student's home situation might be affecting schoolwork. In most situations, I do not exclude these students from participating because I want a fulfilling conversation with their peers to be a motivating force in their desire to do the reading. But there are exceptions, and sometimes I ask a student to leave the instructional conversation. Instead of participating in the rich and interesting discussion, they are to read the material at their seat and write a two- to three-page report. This exclusion can be a motivating force for certain students.

Assessing Instructional Conversations

The teacher is responsible for assessing, formally or informally, where students are at and helping them develop new understandings or knowledge. During the school year, our heads are filled with lesson plan ideas, administrative responsibilities, telephone calls that need to be made to parents, supplies that need to be ordered, and mental notes about who is doing well and who is falling behind. We have grade books, and some of us keep a notepad nearby to add to the ever-expanding "Things to Do" list. Realizing that we are already overloaded, we nevertheless encourage teachers to do one more thing: during or after the instructional conversation, jot down notes next to the students' names on a class roster about their participation and their thinking. These notes are valuable in assessing students' overall performance. We can also quickly learn who is and who is not integrating the ideas covered in the instructional conversation.

In addition, teachers can assess students' understandings by having them complete a product, such as an individual or group report about the subject after the instructional conversation. At the end of Sarah's instructional conversation in lesson 1, she asks the students to go back to their chart that compares and contrasts the different cultures and preservation methods. She requests that they review it and add any ideas that have evolved from the instructional conversation. Students also expand their description of preservation processes to include the concept of resurrection. With contributions by Anne, one of the students, they discuss the future implications of cryonics. In a similar manner, Laura Ianacone Taschek in lesson 2 requires students to compare their initial responses to the new ideas they have developed after participating in the instructional conversation.

Lessons from the Classroom

The following lessons illustrate how three teachers integrate the instructional conversation into their teaching. In lesson 1, Sarah and Albert, long-time friends and colleagues, work together to plan a unit that captures students' enthusiasm. Using the Science Standard of "Science as Inquiry," they focus on forensic science and death. They use the instructional conversation sequence to discuss and compare rituals around death in present and ancient times. Laura Ianacone Taschek weaves the instructional conversation into her unit on war and conflict in lesson 2. Students discuss international war crimes and human rights. All three teachers are invigorated by their students' response and participation in the conversations.

Lesson 1: Biology, Grades 10 and 11

Sarah and Albert, ten-year veteran high school science teachers, state that their year-long teaching goal is to incorporate more student discussion into their curriculum. They identify themselves as "excellent lecturers, proficient graders, and above-average lesson plan writers." They set their goal: to integrate the instructional conversation into their teaching.

Like so many other teachers, they note their students' interest in forensic science television shows. Although not avid TV watchers themselves, they notice that some of their students reference and chat about the newest cases before the first class period begins. Obviously interested and excited about the topics, the students speak with great animation. Sarah and Albert decide to make the most out of their enthusiasm. Using the National Science Education Standards as a starting point in their lesson designs, they set out to create a meaningful, appealing unit that has its origins in student interest.

In their original version of the lesson, the primary vehicle for instruction was lecture. Sarah and Albert quickly recognized that they were not meeting their goal of incorporating small-group instructional conversations into their teaching. They realized that in order to incorporate small-group discussions, they needed to reduce the lecture time, involve their students in researching some of the topics, and provide a simulated investigation. In addition, they needed to work out a schedule to accommodate small-group discussions into their sixty-minute class period.

Sarah wanted the lesson to generate the "Aha" moments she recalls from working in her daughter's sixth-grade classroom when they had literature study groups. She recollects that the students would read a couple of chapters from a book, answer several questions in a writing log, and then meet in a small group to discuss the text and their answers. She states, "I remember being impressed because the quality of the discussion was so high. They really thought about the book's concepts. I could see the kids moving from a beginning understanding of the book to a more developed one."

Albert and Sarah summarized their thoughts by stating, "An instructional conversation is a blending of a great, inspirational, thought-provoking conversation with clear, standards-driven instructional goals." They recognized that the quality of questions needs to be high, challenging students to think in cognitively complex ways. At the same time, the teacher needs to be an astute and attentive listener in order to hear what students understand and what they have yet to master.[9]

Lesson: Forensic Science

Time Estimate: Six to eight 60-minute class periods

National Science Standards

1. Science as Inquiry: Standards support discussions of scientific material so that concepts are analyzed, developed, clarified, reflected upon, and evaluated.

2. The standard of Science and Technology addresses the methods of investigation and analysis of evidence.[10]

Learning Objectives

1. Students consider and write about their thoughts and feelings about death. They compare their thoughts and feelings from the beginning of the unit to the end.

2. Students create charts comparing and contrasting different cultures and preservation methods.

3. Students participate in an instructional conversation. They weave what they learn in the discussion into their final essay.

4. Students research death and preservation processes including mummification and cryonics.

5. Students prepare a PowerPoint presentation sharing their research findings with the class.

Lesson Plan

1. Students consider the following questions:

   - "Everyone ponders death—an inevitable part of the cycle of life. Have you thought about your own death?"

   - "What are your thoughts about death?"

   - "Have you talked with your parents, other family members, or friends about your thoughts?"

   - "Do your culture and/or religion require you to think a certain way or perform certain rituals? What are those?"

   - "What would you like done with your body after you die?"

   Using these questions, they write an essay documenting their thoughts and family rituals about death.

2. Students read articles on the preservation methods of different cultures: mummification, accidental mummification, modern mummification, and cryonic suspension.

3. Students work with a partner to take notes on the readings and create a chart that compares and contrasts (1) the different cultures and (2) preservation methods.

4. Students create a class chart documenting their findings. Every pair of students will be responsible for contributing a specific section as well as adding additional details to other students' sections.

5. Instructional conversation: Each student will participate in an instructional conversation comparing the process of cryonics to mummification and discussing the impact of each on a society's culture.

6. Students are responsible for rereading their original essay. They continue their essay by comparing and contrasting their beliefs and ideas with the readings as well as the information they gained from participating in the instructional conversation.

   Students consider these instructional conversation follow-up questions:

   - Would you still be buried or cremated, or would you prefer to be mummified or placed into cryostasis? Explain your decision.

   - How are you making this decision?

   - Discuss why you are not interested in the other alternative(s).

   - How much influence do you think your friends, family, culture, and religion have on your decision?

7. The teacher gives a mini-lecture/PowerPoint presentation discussing forensic science and how archaeologists interpret clues to learn about a mummy and its culture. Use the example of the "Iceman," who was discovered in the Alps in 1991 by German hikers. The Iceman is thought to have died around 3000 B.C. He is one of the oldest and best preserved mummies ever found.

   Among the key points of the mini-lecture are that by deciphering clues through the use of X rays, CT scans, autopsies, DNA testing, and carbon dating, we can learn about a mummy's age, gender, diseases, cause of death, physical characteristics, religion, and culture. Also, studying the artifacts buried with the mummy gives us information about the culture and religion.

8. In groups of two or three, students will conduct forensic science research. They will be responsible for researching how archaeologists interpreted clues to learn about a specific mummy, such as the famous Tutankhamen or Rameses the Great. Students can also research lesser-known but fascinating mummies such as the Lemon Grove Girl or Juanita, the Ice Maiden. The Lemon Grove Girl and an infant were discovered by two teenage boys in 1966 in a cave near Chihuahua, Mexico. They were stored for fourteen years in Lemon Grove, California. It is believed that the mummies died between A.D. 1040 and 1260. Juanita, also known as the Ice Maiden, was discovered in the Peruvian Andes in 1995 by Johann Reinhard. She was a young Inca girl believed to have died about five hundred years ago.

   Discuss how archaeologists, radiologists, pathologists, botanists, anthropologists, and other scientists determine age, gender, diseases, causes of death, physical characteristics, culture, and religion. The groups will deliver a PowerPoint presentation about their mummy and its characteristics to other class members. (Graphics and other visual illustrations are required.)

Conduct of Lesson

The following dialogue documents the instructional conversation. Note that Sarah uses the Instructional Conversation Sequence from Exhibit 5.1 to guide the conversation and achieve her goals of having students access their own knowledge base and compare the processes and rituals of death.

1. *Connection question:* Ask students to describe or explain some event or experience in their own life that relates to the subject matter. This is how the conversation goes in Sarah's cryonics lesson:

> **Teacher:** At the beginning of this unit, you were asked to ponder death and think about what you want to happen to your body after you die. Now you've read several articles about different preservation practices. Let's share with each other what we want to have happen to our bodies when we die. How are you making this decision? What role do your friends, family, culture, and religion have on your decision?
>
> **Adrienne:** Well, my family believes in burial. My cousin just died, and we had the whole open casket thing with the viewing. My family thinks it is so important. It is kind of creepy though. I was thinking about how gross the

mummification process is, and then I started thinking about the open casket thing, and on some level, they are both pretty gruesome. When I was reading about the Chinchoros, I was appalled at how they disassembled their corpses and chemically treated the bodies. And then I was thinking about *Six Feet Under* and what morticians do to dead bodies, and it's not much different.

Emily: I like cremation. I definitely want to be cremated even though it is against our religion.

Adrienne: What religion is that?

Emily: Jewish.

Adrienne: Why don't they allow cremation?

Emily: I am not exactly sure. But I know it is against the Torah. And my family believes that cremation burns up the person's soul.

Phillip: I want to be put in cryonic suspension and have the chance to come back some day.

Juan: Not me. I don't wanna come back. Besides, that is for the rich folk. Did you read about the cost? Just like the mummies—that was for the rich folk too. I guess some things never change.

Emily: You are so cynical, Juan. So what do you want to happen to your body?

Juan: I don't care, 'cause when you are dead, you're dead.

Teacher: Abe, Anne, or Mai, would you like to share?

Abe: I saw this show about Tibet. And after a person died, they held this week-long ceremony. The body was all wrapped up, and they used some type of embalming liquid. After the week, though, these holy priests cut up the body and fed it to the birds. It was kind of creepy and cool at the same time.

Emily: What do you mean cool? That is disgusting!

Abe: I don't know. I mean, it is just done then. It's over. We become part of the food chain. There is some poetic justice in that. I like thinking that one day, my body could be food for birds.

Mai: My family prefers that we are cremated. We strongly believe in reincarnation.

2. *Weaving question:* Pose a question that requires students to think about how their own experience and knowledge relates to the material. In Sarah's instructional conversation, she inquires:

Teacher: How do you think that your preferences for burial or cremation or death compare to how people felt back in ancient Egypt or Chile or Alaska?

Abe: Like Juan was saying, it was about status, money, and it's still about status. The people who have money still get to have the most choices and the best options.

3. *Text support:* Ask students to provide supporting evidence for their ideas with references from the text:

> **Teacher:** What from the text supports the processes of preservation being about money?
>
> **Juan:** Come on—look on the last page of the cryonics reading. How much does it cost? (Pause as he looks it up.) Fifty to $120,000. That is beaucoup bucks. Or it says that you can list different cryonics companies on your insurance policy, and then the cryonics company gets all the insurance money.
>
> **Emily:** (Murmur) I was just listed as my aunt's beneficiary.
>
> **Juan:** What?
>
> **Emily:** Well, my aunt is really sick, and she just told me that she listed me as her beneficiary. So I get some of her stuff if she dies.
>
> **Adrienne:** That is so sad.
>
> **Emily:** When my little cousin died, her parents buried her with lots of her things, like toys and her favorite blanket and bottle.
>
> **Teacher:** In the articles, they talked about how the Egyptian mummies would sometimes bury their loved ones with furniture, statues, and food for the afterlife. And the Incas buried their dead with food, clothing, and gold.
>
> **Abe:** Yeah, like they talked about the Spanish conquering the Incas and then destroying the burial mounds to pillage the gold.
>
> **Teacher:** So why do you think that for at least the past five thousand years, we have been giving so much of our attention to the dead?
>
> **Mai:** It is like with my family. It is about finding a way to bring the person back.
>
> **Teacher:** From the readings, what makes you think that?
>
> **Phillip:** In the *Nova* article, it calls them Ka (vital force) and Ba (personality). Ka and Ba could reenter the body if they could preserve it. It is about bringing the body and spirit back together. That was their ticket.
>
> **Mai:** Just like reincarnation.
>
> **Juan:** I still think it's all hocus-pocus. We just can't deal with death—the inevitability of an infinite end. No more. A vast nothingness. Seems like we could never deal with it.
>
> **Anne:** I think we are obsessed with it because we are dealing with a huge concept: the concept of eternal life. If I was dying, I would want to extend my life. Wouldn't it truly be amazing to come back if, let's say, I had a terminal illness? I could be cryo-frozen and then come back when they found a cure. Or what if I could be frozen and then come back to meet future generations of my family, like my great-great-grandchildren?

Juan: Okay, that would be cool. But the Egyptians thought that becoming mummified would help them come back. What if this cryonics stuff is simply a modern version of the same old thing?

Phillip: Yeah, the Egyptians really thought that they could come back. One of the scientists said that they thought they could literally get up and go!

Juan: Yeah, and my point is, what if this expensive cryonics thing is really just like that: a way of denying the inevitability of death. Instead of eternal life, eternal nothingness.

Adrienne: You are so depressing, Juan.

Emily: But what if he's wrong? And what if we could come back? Die and come back to do things.

Anne: Yes, like what if we could use cryonics as a protest statement?

Emily: What do you mean?

Anne: A protest against man-made environmental disasters or overpopulation. You could die and come back to see how much progress our culture has made. Are we thinking differently about our environment? Do we get the problem of overpopulation? What if Aristotle could live today? Think how much he could contribute now? Or Einstein.

Teacher: How does cryonics compare to the process of mummification?

Mai: Well, they are both about preservation. A way to preserve the body and spirit.

Abe: It seems to me it's more about resurrection. Cryonic technology promises to bring you back from the dead. A frozen state of death.

Juan: They are both about status. You gotta have money.

Teacher: What is the impact of both these processes on our culture?

Adrienne: It seems that both are about eternity. Creating an eternal memory.

Juan: Yeah, eternal money, wealth, and power. The rich always have had the most choices. Back then and even now.

Emily: You know, Juan, the article mentioned a certain tribe of people who mummified everyone.

Anne: If cryonic technology is advanced enough to work, this could have a huge impact. We can preserve geniuses who could help us down the line with life-threatening problems such as global disease, climatic changes such as global warming, overpopulation, lack of food resources, on and on.

Juan, Phillip: That could be cool. Yeah—something to think about.

4. *Joint product:* Sarah and her students have created a product together. In this instructional conversation, the product is intangible. They verbally compare the two preservation processes of cryonics and mummification. They also could have made the product tangible by documenting the information in chart form.

5. *Homework/seatwork:* Sarah sent the students away with some follow-up work to the discussion:

> **Teacher:** I would like you to go back to your chart that compares and contrasts the different cultures and preservation methods. Please reread it, and add any ideas that came out of this discussion. Please note directly on your chart that these specific ideas came from the instructional conversation. Who can give one example of something that came out of this conversation that you did not really think about from the readings?
>
> **Mai:** Definitely the concept of resurrection.
>
> **Adrienne:** We could add a column for Christianity there, with the whole belief in the resurrection and all.
>
> **Teacher:** It would be fine to add this.
>
> **Phillip:** This conversation has expanded how I have thought about mummies and the cultural congruities between ancient preservation practices and cryonics.

Commentary on Lesson

Sarah and Albert use the instructional conversation focus questions as a framework to evaluate the lesson. Sarah comments on the instructional conversation:

> I am pleased with the high amount of student participation. The students really talk about their ideas. I thought they might clam up since we have never done this in a small group before, and having Albert observe the lesson could be even more intimidating for them. But they jumped right in, sharing their ideas. My biggest challenges are keeping quiet, asking those effective, higher-order questions, and letting them speak. I think I did pretty well! The organizational sequence helps me a ton. I don't think the conversation would have been as productive without the connecting and weaving questions and requiring text support. When Emily started talking about her young cousin, I thought, *There it goes. We are going to end up in a counseling session.*

Notice how Sarah weaves the conversation and Emily's experience right back into the lesson, commenting how the Egyptians and Incas practiced the same ritual of burying their beloved with personal belongings. The quality of questions is critical to having a productive instructional conversation. Albert praises Sarah for the quality of her questions:

• How do you think that your preferences for burial or cremation or death compare to how people felt back in ancient Egypt or Chile or Alaska?

- What from the text supports the processes of preservation being about money?
- So why do you think that for at least the past five thousand years, we have been giving so much of our attention to the dead?
- How does cryonics compare to the process of mummification?

After reviewing and reflecting on the questions, Sarah and Albert recognize that the questions are open-ended and cognitively challenging. They require students to compare and contrast ancient and modern times. Students must make judgments about their ideas using supporting evidence from the text. The questions push past literal comprehension and require analysis, evaluation, and synthesis.

The instructional conversation had a content goal and a language goal. Sarah and Albert determined the goals based on the subject area, the students' language needs, and the teaching objectives. Sarah is satisfied with achieving her goals. She comments, "With high school students who are taking our science classes, I focus on the content. I need to follow a standards-based curriculum, and I need to accomplish many goals before they leave my class. In an instructional conversation, the language goals that I feel comfortable reaching have to do with vocabulary acquisition. I want them to learn and be able to apply scientific vocabulary and concepts."

Lesson 2: Global Studies, Grades 10 to 12

This lesson, contributed by Laura Ianacone Taschek, provides a strong example of a teacher using the state standards to compose interesting questions that stimulate a provocative discussion and writing assignment. It includes a lesson design plan, student assignments, documentation of the instructional conversation, and examples of student work.

During her twelfth-grade Global Issues class, Laura creates a set of centers revolving around four student-chosen themes: Terrorism, Human Rights, Global Environment, and War/Conflict. In one of the centers, the Global Reading Center: War/Conflict, she conducts an instructional conversation to discuss war crimes. Her intention is for the students to share and develop their definition of war crimes and discuss how the international or local community should respond to them. In this guided conversation, she activates students' prior knowledge, drawing on their previous exposure to conversations about their own human rights. She aspires to include more student than teacher talk time. This type of conversational teaching helps her students develop new concepts and apply new language as they discuss the United Nations categories of war crimes: genocide, violations of "the laws of customs of war," and "crimes against humanity."

Table 5.2 illustrates the lesson design plan for the instructional conversation. Notice how the subject matter content addresses the California History Standards.

TABLE 5.2. GLOBAL ISSUES LESSON DESIGN

Big Ideas	Student and Family Knowledge	Skills/Standards	Assessment	Instructional Strategies/ Practices	Resources/ Materials
What are the enduring understandings/essential questions to be addressed?	How will you draw on their ideas, interests, and experiences to connect students to the big ideas?	What important skills/standards will students learn, practice, and apply?	What is meaningful evidence that students have understood the big ideas and reached proficiency on skills/standards?	What instructional practices and strategies will support students to meet the standards and grasp the big ideas?	What resources will best convey the big ideas and concepts that support skill attainment?
What is a war crime? How is it defined?	Contextualize: • Ask students to think about a time in their life when something seemed unfair. • Have you ever gotten away with something?	California History—Social Studies Framework Participation Skills: • Develop group interaction skills. • Develop social and political participation skills.	Students participate in small group instructional conversation facilitated by teacher.	Instructional conversation—small group with teacher present	*Scholastic Update* Magazine's article "What Is a War Crime"
Should the international community hold people or governments responsible/accountable for war atrocities such as genocide?	Make Connections: • Use instructional conversation to connect their experiences with the case studies in the reading.	Ethical Literacy: • Recognize the sanctity of life and the dignity of the individual. • Understand the ways in which different societies have tried to resolve ethical issues. • Realize that concerns for ethics and human rights are universal and represent the aspirations of men and women in every time and place.	Students respond to questions that follow case-study summaries. Students respond to the meta-cognitive questions. Students research further war crimes articles and write an analytical summary.	Learning center activities	Further newspaper articles on the same topic

Source: McGinty, I. (2000). *Unit planning matrix.* Watsonville, CA. This matrix was constructed as a planning guide for the teachers at Starlight Professional Development School. It was developed from Wiggins, G., & McTighe, J. (1998). *Understanding by design.* Alexandria, VA: Association for Supervision and Curriculum Development. The standards are adapted from: California Department of Education. (1998, October). History—Social Science Content Standards for California Public Schools. http://www.cde.ca.gov/board/pdf/history.pdf.

Lesson: War and Conflict
Instructional Conversation

Time Estimate: One week of 90-minute class periods

National Standards for Social Sciences

Students will know and be able to discuss:

- How post–World War II reconstruction occurred and new international power relations took shape.

- The search for community, stability, and peace in an interdependent world.[11]

Learning Objectives

1. Students will participate in an instructional conversation to discuss international war crimes.

2. Students will evaluate and judge whether the criminals should be held accountable many years after the crimes were committed.

Lesson Plan

1. Each student reads and responds to the *Scholastic Update* article, "What Is a War Crime?"[12]

2. Students respond to the questions that follow the article asking students to contemplate whether society should hold people and the government accountable for war crimes. Students work with the issue of closure: When have a country and its people been punished and suffered enough?

3. Each student participates in an instructional conversation.

4. After the instructional conversation, reread your answers to the text questions. Compare your original responses to the new ideas you have developed after participating in the instructional conversation. Students can refer to Handout 5.1 for more detail.

————————————————

Conduct of Lesson

On page 117 is an example of excerpts from one of Laura's instructional conversations. Laura uses the Instructional Conversation Sequence in Exhibit 5.1 to structure the conversation. For many of Laura's students, this is their first attempt at participating in an instructional conversation. Consequently, the discussions can be slow to start. With some prompting, Laura witnesses excellent examples of higher-level reasoning and speaking. Many students are quite articulate and passionate about the topic.

Handout 5.1
Student Assignment for the Global Reading Center Human Rights Task: What Is a War Crime?

Prior to meeting in your assigned group (A, B, C, D, and E), please do the following assignment.

1. Read the handout in the folder titled "What Is a War Crime?" Read the introduction, page 1. While you are reading, choose three vocabulary words that have to do with war crimes. Write down each word and a definition on your paper. (A dictionary may be checked out at the front of the classroom.) Choose one of these words, and create a graphic or illustration of what the word means. (You have creative license!)

2. After the introduction, there are three current cases of alleged war crimes in Bosnia, France, and Guatemala. Read each case, and think about the questions at the end of the article. Take a few minutes to write responses to the questions. Be sure to explain and support your opinion with text references.

3. Be prepared to discuss the article when you attend your scheduled instructional conversation. You will be discussing the questions at the end of each short article on the second page of the handout. Please bring your article, your written responses, and your well-read self to the group meeting.

4. Following the instructional conversation, be prepared to compare your original responses to the new ideas you have developed after participating in the instructional conversation. Please respond to the following meta-cognitive questions:

   • How have your views changed?

   • How have you further developed your thinking?

   • What new questions have arisen?

   • How has your understanding of the complexity of the situation changed?

1. *Connection question:* The conversation begins with some questions to help the students contextualize the discussion on war crimes. Laura is assessing students' previous personal experience of this subject. She asks students to recount a time when they thought something unfair had happened to them. She provides an initial example, and then students begin sharing their stories:

> **Teacher:** First, I want you to think about an example of when you felt something unfair happened to you. You can use an example from your childhood, from school, or from your friends.
>
> **Student:** Well . . . I remember when I was little, I was the oldest, and I always got blamed for things that I didn't do.
>
> **Teacher:** Can you give an example?
>
> **Student:** Once my brother and I were at home, and my parents were gone. We were watching TV, and my brother came up and started wrestling with me. Then I knocked down a lamp on the table, and it broke into lots of pieces. When my parents got home, my brother blamed me. And even though I knocked over the lamp, it was he who started wrestling with me. I thought it was unfair that I got blamed for it. He didn't even get in trouble.

Following this question, Laura reverses the idea and asks, "Have you ever gotten away with something?" After some general devious laughter, the students provide examples of incidents when they felt they got away with something. They also discuss how people on each side of the situation might feel.

2. *Weaving question:* Once the students share their own experiences, Laura asks them how their stories relate to the case studies about war crimes in the reading:

> **Teacher:** In what way do the experiences we just talked about relate to the article and the cases cited in the article?
>
> **Student 1:** In the case study about the French policeman, he was being blamed for killing the Jews and he didn't think it was his fault. I don't know . . . I mean the police guy said he was ordered to do it. He was doing what he was ordered to do. Maybe he was scared that he would get shot.
>
> **Student 2:** Yeah, but I don't think that is an excuse for what he did. He was working with the Nazis, collaborating to send the Jews to concentration camps!
>
> **Teacher:** In what way, if any, is the policeman's experience similar to our personal examples?
>
> **Student 1:** Well, he was getting blamed for something that he didn't think was his fault. Like I didn't think that the lamp breaking was my fault.

Student 2: Yeah, but couldn't you say that the lamp breaking was sort of your fault and your brother's fault? It was both of your faults.

Student 1: Well . . . I guess.

Teacher: How did you feel about getting blamed?

Student 1: Not good at all. I was mad. I thought it was unfair.

Teacher: How do you think the French policeman felt?

Student 1: Kinda like me, like it was unfair. I don't know if he was angry, though. But it doesn't sound as if he wants to go to jail. But what he did, it was kinda messed up. I helped break a lamp; he was doing something that killed people.

Teacher: Excellent point. Should he be held accountable for his actions even if he was being ordered by the government?

Student 4: Yes, absolutely.

Student 1: But he might have been killed if he didn't obey.

Student 5: This is messed up. I don't know. It's messed up.

Teacher: Let's talk about what the crime was and maybe explore what parts of it he should be accountable for.

3. *Text support:* Laura notices that while keeping her own talking to a minimum, she needs to interject questions and comments to keep the discussion going. During one such instance, she asks the students whether they think people should be held accountable for war crimes. She also asks them to use evidence from the reading to support their point of view:

Teacher: Should people be held accountable for war crimes?

Student 1: Yes! I think so.

Student 2: Well . . . it depends on the situation. What's going on in the country?

Teacher: Can you elaborate? Could you give an example from one of the case studies?

Student 2: Well, in the case from Guatemala, it says that about "150,000 Indians were killed, 1 million driven from their homes, and 50,000 more simply disappeared." It says that the old government was responsible for the killing, but now that there is a new government, they want to stir it all up and punish the people from the old government for what they did.

Teacher: Who are they?

Student 2: The . . . Truth Commission, who is supposed to document the human rights violations. They work for the new government.

Student 1: Yeah, I agree with the Truth Commission. They want to hold these old government people responsible for what they did. They should. They killed a lot of people.

Student 3: Yeah, but the case study also says that if they grant . . . what is it? Umm . . . amnesty, that would be the best to put the civil war behind them.

Student 1: But what about all the victims? That doesn't seem fair to their families.

Student 3: Yeah, but if they start accusing people, maybe the violence will happen again. It is like the other center activity. The one where we talked about what is going on in Northern Ireland. What's going to stop them from taking out their guns and killing people again to get revenge?

4. *Joint product:* The students continue to talk about the advantages and disadvantages to the Truth Commission's policy of not naming specific names. Although no consensus is reached about what the Guatemalan government should do, the students are engaged in a stimulating and thought-provoking discussion.

5. *Homework/seatwork:* The students are required to complete step 4 of the student assignment (see Handout 5.1) where they compare their original responses to the new ideas they have developed after participating in the instructional conversation.

Lesson Assessment

When Laura conducts an instructional conversation, first she has students write their answers to questions from the text. After the discussion, she asks them to think about the ideas of the other students, review their initial responses, and compose a new answer. She requests they compare their old answer to the new one and respond to the meta-cognitive questions. (See Handout 5.1.)

Another form of assessment involves research. For this instructional conversation, students conduct research on a current war crime in the news. At the time Laura's class was doing this assignment, there were reports in the news about a Guatemalan priest who had been killed. Many students opted to research this topic; others were interested in current events in Asia. Once students locate and read recent articles, the students can either (1) write up a summary and analysis of two or more articles and how the instructional conversation relates to it, or (2) create a visual representation such as a chart or graph and present their work to the class.

Commentary on Lesson

Laura wants her students to walk away from the conversation having thought about criminal injustices from a different perspective. Her content goals move beyond having students define and provide examples of war crimes. She wants students to think about the issues of accountability, fairness, and human dignity. She wants them to evaluate the rationale of war crimes and the consequences on groups of people. She aspires to make the curriculum meaningful to students by having them relate to it. So often history is faraway and inaccessible. She wants students to view it on a more personal level.

The instructional conversation has become a critical part of Laura's teaching. Through the conversation, she assesses what students comprehend and what is still confusing to them. By following the Instructional Conversation Sequence, she connects students' experiences to the readings. She relates, "It is this connection that gives school meaning." Although there surely is no comparison between the Nazi war crimes and the student who was blamed for breaking the lamp, if this experience serves as a springboard for students to deepen their understanding of war crimes, nurture their compassion and empathy for human rights, and question human rights decisions and choices, then we have succeeded in helping our students become thinking, questioning, and literate human beings.

Learning to incorporate instructional conversations into teaching takes practice and patience. We must be willing to engage in much trial and error. Our students can be our teachers, showing us how to construct meaningful questions, leading us to search for ways to link their knowledge and experiences to the new concepts, guiding us in presenting academic English in better and more useful ways, and teaching us how to become better listeners.

Exhibit 5.3 presents two examples of student work from Laura's War and Conflict instructional conversation.

Conclusion

The instructional conversation provides a framework as well as an instructional method that teachers can effectively use to engage adolescents in conversing about important topics. In this chapter, Sarah, Albert, and Laura create standards-driven, academically rigorous lessons. Through the excerpts of instructional conversations, we gain glimpses into the possibilities for student engagement and thoughtful, higher-level thinking. The students themselves illustrate the movement from a superficial to a deep, involved dialogue. We want our students to care about and be involved in school. Consequently, we can facilitate a forum that demands and cherishes their contributions.

EXHIBIT 5.3. SAMPLES OF STUDENT WORK ON THE WAR AND CONFLICT UNIT

Maria's Comments on the Case Study Questions

Suspect: General Efrain Rios Montt

Place: Guatemala

Charge: Genocide

I think that by granting amnesty to the people who committed these atrocities will not help Guatemala move forward. These people destroyed the lives of many innocent and guilty people. If these people aren't held accountable, I believe that this problem could occur in the future. However, there are some advantages to the truth commission's policy of not naming names. The guerillas, who were some of the Mayan's whose rights were being taken away, will not be charged for trying to defend themselves. Instead, they will be able to peacefully start their lives over. The disadvantages to the truth commission's policy is that the government soldiers may think that in the future they may be able to get away with killing the Mayan people.

After the small group discussion I have realized that there is really no easy fix. One person mentioned that the government should be held responsible for the lives they took since they started this terrible civil war. That caught my interest because I began to think of how both parties really are to blame, but the purpose of a government in my eyes is to protect and help a country to survive. In this situation I realize there is not one answer to solve problems for both the government and the people. I have now come to the conclusion that the decision of the truth commission's policy to not name names may essentially be the best answer to this problem, but I also think that the government should try to help out the people whose lives were scarred by this war. They should try to help out those families who lost their loved ones and were put into financial turmoil.

Salvador's Comments on the Global Reading Center's Human Rights Task

The third article, about the French man who arrested Jews and sent them to be killed, I believe with certainty that this is immoral, inhumane genocide, and most certainly it is a war crime. They argue that he was only obeying orders. Well, then, also his superiors are guilty of war crimes.

I see the last question, but I am hesitant to answer it. I have been taught to always forgive, that we live by grace, and that since we are forgiven, so, also we forgive. As much as I can, I try not to judge anything, but today, I see that these were god's people that died. It is written, "Whoever isn't with us for the good of humanity is against." So, I will have to say that these people should be punished, not only the man mentioned in the article, but also his superiors and anyone involved in such hateful, inhuman actions. This cannot happen again. Certain people cannot think that they could get away with such horrible actions. I found this article very disturbing.

So our group met with Ms. Taschek and talked about these war crimes. Although, I have not and will not change my opinion about this man and his superiors being punished, I can see the situation is more complex. Like what if this was me who was being ordered to do something horrible? I think I would run away from my country. If I had a family, I would take them too. I have done a couple of things in my life already where I blamed someone else instead of taking the blame myself. My younger brother took the blame and I feel really bad about this now because I see how this kind of thinking can start. You are too scared to take the responsibility for what you did. I think this French man should just admit what he did, say it was wrong, and be willing to go to prison to pay for his actions.

Most people in the group agreed with me but two people felt like it was so long ago and this guy is so old, we should just forgive and start over again. Like I said before, I don't know if I could forgive such immoral, inhumane actions. I am wondering how many people from WWII are in this guy's shoes—waiting to be punished for their crimes?

Conclusion
A Model of Assistance

We must come to understand that a school is not a school unless
all learn. . . . Ironically, schools will improve only when they . . .
move toward more education for their teachers. Only when
teachers are continually learning will they develop for
themselves a new vision of schooling and teaching.
R. G. Tharp and R. Gallimore, *Rousing Minds to Life: Teaching,*
Learning, and Schooling in Social Context (1988)

It's a cool April morning during spring break, and I am attending a professional development meeting with a group of teachers, principals, educational researchers, and university professors. Also in attendance are several members of the Greenlandic Education Delegation.[1] We have gathered to discuss how to integrate the five principles into our teaching. In addition to joint productive activity, language development, contextualized instruction, complex thinking, and instructional conversation, the delegation from Greenland is adopting two more principles: modeling/demonstration and student choice.[2] They believe these seven principles reflect the heart of teaching and learning. They provide a culturally compatible pedagogy in which the individual and her or his family and community experiences and knowledge are recognized as a vital part of the learning process.

This group animatedly affirms how they desire all their schools to be alive with rich conversations; full of lively, collaborative work; and active with cognitively challenging and stimulating work for all students. As we ponder our visions, the teachers from Greenland discuss the importance of Greenlandic mythology—a mythology whose vision of people as multifaceted beings naturally supports a holistic understanding of how children learn. These teachers consider all aspects of their students: the emotional, social, intellectual, spiritual, and psychological state of the child. The Greenlanders have even gone so far as to create an educational component for healing and compassion.

Would it not behoove our own educational leaders to consider such a holistic view of the child? Would it not be in the best interest of our society to consider this holistic picture of the teacher as well? Granted, our relatively large, diverse, and complex society poses many challenges to educational reform. But my experience working with the five principles in diverse educational settings has convinced me that American schools too can respond to students as whole human beings.

This book began with many questions:

- What are we teaching our students?
- How important is this content material to students' lives?
- How can we draw on our students' prior knowledge and integrate their ideas and experiences into the curriculum?
- How can we capture students' interest and enthusiasm?
- How can we change the statistics about who succeeds and who fails in school?
- How can we offer all our students an equitable education where their needs and desires are met within the school system, within our classrooms?

By using the five principles of teaching and learning presented in this book as a guidepost, teachers can evaluate their curriculum, instruction, and assessments. They can assess how they are teaching using these five principles:

Students and Teachers Producing Together

Developing Literacy and Language Across the Curriculum

Connecting School to Students' Lives

Teaching Complex Thinking

Teaching Through Conversation

For many of us, this type of teaching is not new. However, our commitment to it might be renewed as we consider the ideas presented in the book. This type of teaching requires us to invite our students into the learning process. It demands that we ask our students about themselves: their lives outside school, their families, communities, previous knowledge, and experiences. And it obligates us to let students in on the assessment process. We collaborate with students to develop and discuss how they are performing in relation to specific standards and assessments. We become partners in the learning process.

One of the most important features of these principles is that they provide a model of mutual assistance.[3] In order to succeed as teachers, we must receive support and assistance ourselves. Teachers must be exposed to these five principles in their professional development experiences. Effective professional development demands that we use and apply the same ideas and concepts that we are asking teachers to do with their students. We are thereby modeling and demonstrating the value and effectiveness of the ideas.

After teachers have the opportunity to work collaboratively, discussing these ideas and changing their lesson plans to integrate more student participation and opportunities for language development and complex thinking, they often feel energized about their teaching. Sometimes they feel overwhelmed by all the ideas they want to integrate. The process of changing teaching is an evolution. Like any other process, it involves making small, comfortable changes. I advise teachers to go slowly and to know that sometimes less is more. One of the worst feelings is to put hours of time and energy into integrating new ideas into lessons, units, and teaching and to have few, if any, significant results. I caution teachers to proceed carefully, integrating the principles slowly.

During a recent conference, one group of middle school teachers asked which change I recommend making first. With this particular group of teachers, who were teaching a population of 90 percent Mexican American students, I suggested that they begin to build a component into every lesson where they access their students' knowledge and experiences and weave their experiences to the academic material. It is an effective starting place where you get to know your students as well as express value for their contributions to school. Whether you choose starting at this place or another, such as letting your students know how you will be assessing their work, the point is to begin—to allow ourselves to be beginners in the teaching and learning process.

I leave you with several teachers' comments about the importance of applying these principles in their classrooms. We are developing our base of knowledge so that we can become proficient and automatic in using these principles in our classrooms to create places of deep, meaningful, and heartfelt learning.

> By learning to use these principles, I am being asked about my expertise and experience with teaching and learning. I am not being asked to use the latest repertoire of 'strategies.' I am allowed to create my lesson plans and then review them and rework them to make them better for my students. I feel like my expertise is being used—and appreciated. (Laura)

> How great to be allowed to collaborate with other teachers to plan meaningful lessons and units that I can use and apply and reflect upon. (Elizabeth)

> It is awesome to rework my lessons with my peers and have the activities be meaningful and challenging for my students. We are using what we've already created but changing it to make it better. This is the best use of my time. And I believe my knowledge base is growing exponentially. I am learning how to ask effective questions, get my students interested in the material, learn what is important to them and how to integrate it into my teaching. (Albert)

To sit in small groups and discuss important ideas is fulfilling, stimulating, rejuvenating. I consider myself intellectual, and instructional conversations provide a great way to consider, judge, evaluate, analyze, and ponder ideas. (Alaina)

Continuing to build my language and conceptual knowledge about teaching and learning has been an intellectual and professional pleasure. I recently had a discussion with my veterinarian. I realized that she has to complete hours of further training every year to stay current with the newest procedures, tools, discoveries, and accompanying concepts and vocabulary. She is treated like a professional. And now, for the first time in my career, I feel this too. (Sarah)

Appendix 1: Creating and Managing Classroom Learning Centers

Learning centers are an organizational system for integrating joint productive activities into high school classes. They provide students with an array of choices. Students have a certain amount of autonomy about determining their time lines, work partners, specific activities, and the processes they use to accomplish the learning objectives.

Creating centers can be difficult and time-consuming in the beginning, but the results are impressive: rich discussions, passionate essays, interesting and personalized research papers. Center activities provide a successful format for implementing the five principles discussed in this book. Research proves that centers are most effective when the activities and goals contextualize instruction within the students' own experiences, develop language in the subject matter, and offer students cognitively challenging instruction and assessment.[1] They allow the students a self-paced, self-chosen environment while providing time for the teacher to initiate instructional conversations with small groups of students. This type of quality instructional time is becoming more difficult to manage with increasing classroom size, a reality in most classrooms. One of the most important benefits of centers is the one-on-one teacher-student time.

Learning center activities require students and teachers to make a paradigm shift in their thinking about what constitutes teaching and learning. Students need to have an open mind because they are about to experience a different type of learning environment. Both their role and that of the teacher have changed. No longer primarily a lecturer, the teacher becomes a coach and assistant. And students are required to take a more active role in their own learning. Laura Ianacone Taschek recounts, "At first, many of my students complained that moving from center to center, working in groups, actively participating in discussions, and creating tangible products was more than they bargained for. However, once we got started, they became interested in the content as well as the structures."

Learning centers are used for other types of lessons besides joint activities. The teacher designs the center activities based on the learning goals. Some activities are best done in pairs or small groups, such as the castle activity in Chapter One. Other center activities are best accomplished alone, offering students independent practice in specific content areas. Students are able to access each other's expertise to assist with their work within their small groups.

Organizing the Centers

Within a center system, the teacher can have a teacher center for conducting a small-group discussion or instructional conversation about a specific concept related to the unit of study. The other centers represent exemplary joint productive activities where the students must work together, at least for part of the activity. Centers can be inter-disciplinary, involving science, social studies, and history, where the students are required to collaboratively design a project together. Other centers can require the students to write, research, analyze, or solve a problem together. For example, here is how Laura set up learning centers for her World History Middle Ages unit:

> Slide Center: Life of Serfs (The Politics and Economy of Serfdom)
>
> Art Center: Frescos—The Meaning and the Art
>
> Music Center: Christmas Music from the Middle Ages
>
> Reading Center: The Black Death and Its Economic Consequences
>
> Writing Center: The Emergence of Religion—Christianity, Buddhism, and Islam
>
> Video Center: The Emergence of Castles

Laura explains how she introduces learning centers to her class: "At first, we brainstorm the responsibilities of a person in the working world. We discuss production deadlines, meetings, independent work, teamwork, creativity, and even fifteen-minute breaks. This is when I introduce the concept of learning centers. Much of center work requires students to use skills needed in the working world. They need to be independent, meet deadlines, work in teams to accomplish tasks, and have meaningful conversations and constructive meetings."

Many teachers prefer learning centers to be self-contained. This means that the students find the instructions for the activity at the center in a binder labeled

"Learning Center Activity Instructions," framed in a picture frame that is standing up on the table, or laminated and on the table. Provide a folder with extra copies of the instructions so that each participant may have a copy. Accompanying the learning center instructions is a basket or box of needed materials. As the groups rotate through the centers, they will find everything they need at each center. Teachers can allow anywhere from thirty to sixty minutes at each center depending on the teaching goals. Consequently, a class can spend five to ten days on one set of learning centers so that all of the students can rotate through all of the centers.

Classroom Groupings

There are many ways to organize the groups to rotate through the centers. Teachers can randomly select heterogeneous groups using a number count-off: all the 1's rotate through the centers together, all the 2's work together, and so forth. Or they can select heterogeneous or homogeneous groups based on a specific criterion, such as ability level (match higher-performing with lower-performing students), language dominance (match higher-performing English Language Learners with newer English Language Learners), or learning style (match spatial with highly verbal or mathematically minded students). In this way, each student brings strength and skill to the group. It is useful to organize groups homogeneously if you are targeting instruction on a specific concept or skill. For example, a teacher might have one group of students who require extra support in learning about algebraic equations in mathematics. They can also allow students to self-select their groups based on friendship or social compatibility. Allow students to choose the centers they would like to attend. Arrange six or seven chairs at each table; once the chairs are filled, the center is closed. This is how the students will rotate through all the subsequent centers: by choice.

With high school students, most teachers find it best to allow the group to decide which center they would like to attend. At certain times, it is pertinent for students to complete the centers in a specific order. For example, teachers can ask students to go to a specific follow-up center after they meet for the instructional conversation. However, it is easier not to have the follow-up center so that the order in which students rotate is not relevant.

Group Management and Discipline

Cooperative learning activities require students to work in pairs or small groups to complete an activity. The teacher delivers the instructions and answers preliminary questions. Classic problems that occur include one or two students doing most of the work, the students receiving a mediocre grade because not everyone "gave it their all," and operating in a chaotic classroom environment where everyone is chatting but little productive work seems to be happening.

A decade ago, Spencer Kagan wrote that one of the most neglected, but most critical, topics in cooperative learning was classroom management.[2] It is critical for teachers to consider what their management system will be when they use joint activities. What are the responsibilities and rights of each student? What will the consequences be if students cannot work peacefully with each other? How can we use conflict resolution and mediation tools to help work with conflict in a productive and meaningful way?

Managing joint activities uses a different set of skills from managing a classroom to deliver a lecture. Teachers need to be concerned with arranging groups and seating, controlling the level of sound and activity within the classroom, modeling the activity, giving verbal and written directions, setting up systems for distributing and storing materials, and building students' repertoire of social skills.[3]

Just as it is critical to have an organized management system in a traditional classroom setting, so it is true in a classroom operating with joint activities or learning centers. One teacher, Angelina, and several of her colleagues found it helpful to discuss and create a chart of rights and responsibilities for activity center work time. Collaborating with students to construct such a chart ensures more student ownership. These rights and responsibilities reflect their values and priorities. The chart in Table A-1.1 was created in collaboration with one group of students.

TABLE A-1.1. LEARNING CENTER RIGHTS AND RESPONSIBILITIES

Rights	*Responsibilities*
We have the right to talk with our peers about our work and ask them for help.	We have the responsibility to talk quietly with our friends. Be respectful of them. Be collaborative, not distracting.
We have the right to use all the materials and resources necessary to complete our work.	We have the responsibility to use the materials and resources in a respectful manner in order to finish our work.
We have the right to work at our own pace to finish our work.	We have the responsibility to complete our work on the due date. If this means we need to do it at home, we'll do it.
We have the right to ask questions and voice concerns to our peers and the teacher.	We have the responsibility to make our voice heard in a positive and appropriate manner. (No put-downs or screaming please.)

Source: Adapted from Leal School, Urbana, Illinois, 1984.

Scheduling Center Activities

Since some students enjoy lecture and it serves as a vehicle for delivering information, many teachers continue to incorporate mini-lectures and discussions into their teaching. For example, two days a week, a teacher could lecture on the same theme that is addressed in the learning centers. Some of the discussions can continue to be whole-group, weaving in cooperative small-group strategies because this ensures more equitable student participation. Here is an example of how Laura schedules her history course:

Learning Center and Lecture Schedule

Monday	Center Activities
Tuesday	Mini-Lecture and Discussion
Wednesday	Center Activities
Thursday	Mini-Lecture and Discussion
Friday	Center Activities

Teachers need to plan the goals and how to assess if these objectives have been met. They need to determine the activities, groups and seating, comfortable sound and activity levels, verbal and written instructions, materials distribution and storage, and acceptable behaviors. All of these factors have to be planned and designed in order for learning centers to operate effectively for students. Many teachers involve their students in the process of making these decisions, as this contribution encourages student participation and enthusiasm.

Learning Center Assessment

All teachers are concerned about the issue of accountability. What do we do with students who do not or will not collaborate? And how do we grade students on their individual accomplishments in a collective setting?

Before breaking students into groups to rotate through the centers, it is helpful to preview each activity by reviewing the goals and the procedures for completing the tasks.

In order to make students accountable for their work at each center, teachers can require them to take careful notes about their experiences. Each day they must document their experience by writing a journal entry describing their work. They must write what they accomplished, new ideas or concepts they learned, what was challenging, and where they will begin their work the next time. Laura also uses a grade and criteria sheet to keep track of her students' progress through the centers. An example used in her World History Middle Ages Unit is shown in Exhibit A-1.1.

EXHIBIT A-1.1. MIDDLE AGES GRADE AND CRITERIA SHEET

Center	Name of Activity	Date Started	Date Completed	Total Points Earned

In addition, Laura always hands out copies of the assessments so that her students can review how they are evaluated on each activity. She informs them of the end-of-the-unit evaluation that follows after everyone has rotated through all of the learning centers. It might be an exam, a portfolio of their center work, or a presentation, depending on the goals of the unit.

Conclusion

Learning centers offer high school teachers another option in planning meaningful curriculum and instruction. They require teachers and students to collaborate as partners in the learning process. They simulate the real-world work environment where students carry much of the responsibility for meeting goals, setting time lines, and negotiating with their peers. Finally, they offer teachers a way to integrate the five principles of collaborative learning, language development, contextualized instruction, complex thinking, and instructional conversations into their classroom practice.

Appendix 2: Laurellos Castle

Laurellos Castle

Castle Location

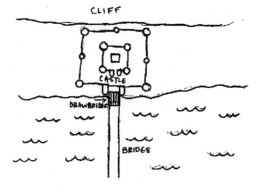

General Info.

Outer Curtain
- 350ft. long sides
- 20ft. high, 8ft. thick
- topped with battlements
- 7 towers, 30ft. high, conical roofs
- Gatehouse, chain-raised drawbridge, portcullis, 2 heavy wood and iron doors

Outer Ward
Used as running ground for horses, practice ground for garrison, and festival grounds

Inner Curtain
- 200ft. long sides
- 35ft. high, 12ft. thick
- topped with battlements
- 4 towers, 50ft. high, conical roofs
- Gatehouse, portcullis, 2 heavy wood and iron doors

Inner Ward
Living quarters and work area, includes Keep, chapel and well

1,2 &3—The Keep

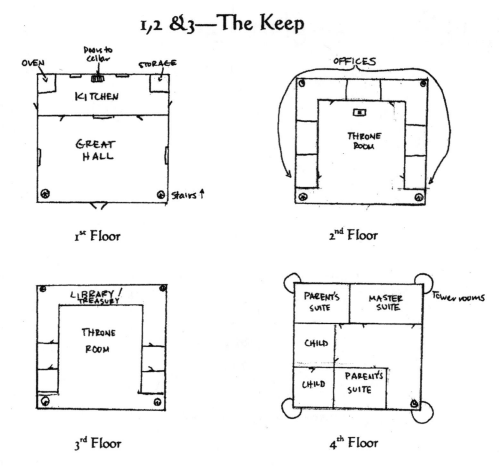

1st Floor

2nd Floor

3rd Floor

4th Floor

Great Hall—used as main dining room for castle inhabitants, long tables arranged around edge of room, high table for Lord and family on raised platform, large windows covered with iron grates, three large fireplaces for heat, center of room left open for entertainment purposes

Kitchen—had large oven and storeroom, cellar below for storing wine and things that spoil, had large fireplaces for roasting meat and central fire with iron sheet hung over it for a stove, water pumped directly into kitchen from cistern built into wall

Throne Room—formal reception area for Lord, two stories high with vaulted ceiling, imported marble floor, walls hung with banners, lg. Windows, raised dais with throne, where local court h ld and where Lord's subjects could bring forth their requests and problems

Offices—for steward and other staff of Lord, and Lord himself, places to work out castle's daily running and financial situation

Library—above offices on balcony, also doubled as treasury

Suites for family—large and luxurious, sm. Towers on each corner, glass windows, fireplaces, walls hung with tapestries and painted, included private gathering area for family to meet, talk, and eat together, rooms for Lord and Lady, their children, and their parents

4—Guest House and Stables

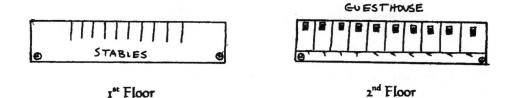

1st Floor   2nd Floor

Stables—had stalls for horses, room for grain, hay and tack

Guest house—had rooms for any minor nobles who visited castle, comfortable rooms

5—Chapel

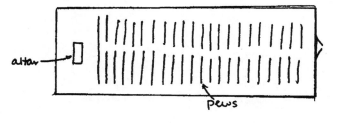

1st Floor

Three story structure with vaulted ceilings, peak roof, and stained glass, where castle occupants worshipped, Lord and family had private pew near altar

6 & 7—Mew and Kennel

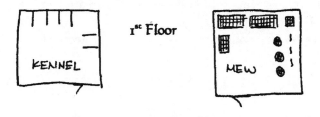

1st Floor

Mew—place where hunting birds kept

Kennel—hunting dogs kept here

8 & 9—Barracks, Blacksmith, and Infirmary

1ˢᵗ Floor   2ⁿᵈ Floor

Blacksmith—repairs metal works, makes weapons, includes room for armory and fletcher

Infirmary—local doctor/herbalist worked here, towsnpeople also came here to be cured, especially important during siege, could be sealed off to keep sickness away from others

Barracks—sm. cell rooms for garrison

10—Inner Towers

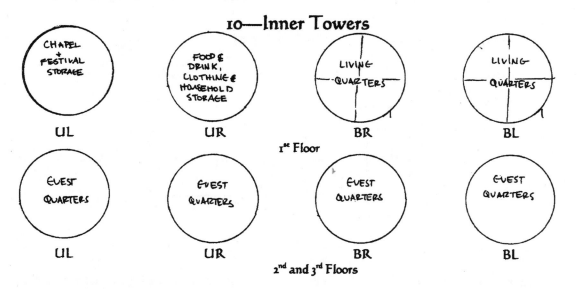

Guest Quarters—for high-ranking guests only

Storage—food and drink, clothing, wagons, rock missles, misc. items

Living Quarters—rooms split between castle servants and staff

Had walkways along walls connecting towers, protected by battlements

11—Outer Towers

Had food, drink, and cots for men defending them during a siege, walkways along walls connected them together at roof level

Other Features

Gardens—small patches of garden on either side of chapel, for beauty and to offer respite, also had fruit trees within to supplement food sources

Well—large pool opening located in front of Keep, supplied water to castle, had cover that went over it to keep water clean

Appendix 3: Tibet Questions Graphic Organizer

Name: _____

Period: _____

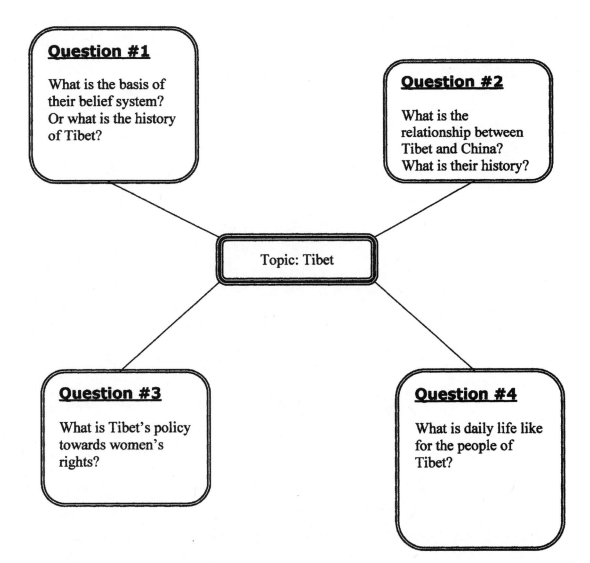

Question #1

What is the basis of their belief system? Or what is the history of Tibet?

Question #2

What is the relationship between Tibet and China? What is their history?

Topic: Tibet

Question #3

What is Tibet's policy towards women's rights?

Question #4

What is daily life like for the people of Tibet?

Notes

INTRODUCTION

1. Stoddart, T. (March 1996). *CCTD report.* Santa Cruz: University of California.

2. Garcia, E. (1999). *Student cultural diversity: Understanding and meeting the challenge.* Boston: Houghton Mifflin.

3. National Clearinghouse for English Language Acquisition and Language Instruction Educational Programs. (2003). *Elementary and secondary LEP demographics.* http:// www.ncela.gwu.edu/.

4. Garcia. (1999).

5. Tharp, R. G., & Gallimore, R. (1988). *Rousing minds to life: Teaching, learning, and schooling in social context.* Cambridge: Cambridge University Press.

6. Kaufman, P., Alt, M. N., & Chapman, C. D. (2002). *Dropout rates in the United States, 2000.* Washington, DC: U.S. Department of Education, National Center for Educational Statistics. http://www.ed/gov/pubs/edpubs/html.

7. Cited in ibid.

8. In this book, I refer to multicultural and equity pedagogy researchers as experts who have extensively studied students placed at risk due to geographical, language, cultural, and socioeconomic factors. They each recommend certain elements to be in place in order to assist minority students in achieving an equitable education. These experts include D. Au, D. August, J. Banks, J. Cummins, L. Delpit, P. Espinoza, P. Friere, R. Gallimore, E. Garcia, M. Gibson, H. A. Giroux, C. Goldenberg, K. Hakuta, S. B. Heath, S. Kagan, J. Kozol, G. Ladson-Billings, E. Lee, I. McGinty, J. Oakes, J. Ogbu, L. Pease-Alvarez, N. Reis, B. Rogoff, C. Sleeter, R. Tharp, L. Villareal, and L. Wong-Fillmore. This is by no means an exhaustive list.

9. Violas, P. C. (1978). *The training of the urban working class: A history of twentieth century American education.* Skokie, IL: Rand McNally.

10. National Commission on Excellence in Education. (1983). *A nation at risk: The imperative for educational reform.* Washington, DC: U.S. Government Printing Office. www.ed.gov/pubs/NatAtRisk/risk.html.

11. Tharp, R. G. (1997). *From at-risk to excellence: Research, theory, and principles for practice.* Santa Cruz: University of California, Santa Cruz, Center for Research on Education, Diversity and Excellence.

12. Center for Research on Education, Diversity and Excellence. (2002). *Research evidence: Five standards for effective pedagogy and student outcomes.* Santa Cruz: University of California, Santa Cruz, Center for Research on Education, Diversity and Excellence.

CHAPTER ONE

1. These cooperative learning strategies belong to the work of Kagan, S. (1994). *Cooperative learning.* San Clements, CA: Kagan Cooperative Learning.

2. Thanks to Jack Mallory for his flexibility, openness, and dedication to new teaching ideas. He allowed Laura to experiment with learning centers in his social studies classes. Then he dedicated himself to creating and implementing a series of learning centers in his own classes.

3. Stahl, R. J. (1994). *The essential elements of cooperative learning in the classroom.* Bloomington. IN: ERIC Clearinghouse for Social Studies/Social Science Education. (ERIC Document Reproduction Service No. ED370881) http://www.ericfacility.net/ericdigets/ed370881.html.

4. Springer, L., Stanne, M. E., & Donovan, S. F. (1999). Effects of small-group learning on undergraduates in science, mathematics, engineering, and technology: A meta-analysis. *Review of Educational Research, 69,* 21–51.

5. U.S. Department of Education, Office of Vocational and Adult Education. (2003, December). *Turning around low-performing high schools: Issue papers, the High School Leadership Summit.* Washington, DC: U.S. Department of Education. http://www.ed.gov/about/offices/list/ovae/pi/hsin it/index.html.

6. August, D. D., & Hakuta, K. (1997). *Improving schooling for language minority children.* Washington, DC: National Academy Press.

7. Kagan. (1994).

8. Center for Research on Education, Diversity and Excellence. (2000). *Pedagogy, research, and practice.* Santa Cruz: University of California, Santa Cruz, Center for Research on Education, Diversity and Excellence.

9. Kagan, S. (1994).

10. These focus questions were developed: (a) in collaboration in the summer of 2003 with Lucia Villareal, a nationally–board certified master teacher at Starlight Elementary School, and (b) from Stephanie Dalton's work: Dalton, S. (1998). *Pedagogy matters: Standards for effective teaching practice.* Santa Cruz, CA: Center for Research on Education, Diversity and Excellence.

11. California Department of Education. (1997, December). Language Arts Content Standards for California Public Schools. http://www.cde.ca.gov.

12. Twain, M. (1981). *The adventures of Huckleberry Finn.* New York: Bantam Books. Hurston, Z. N. (1991). *Their eyes were watching God.* New York: HarperCollins. Crutcher, C. (1995). *Ironman.* New York: Greenwillow Books.

13. California Department of Education. (1998, October). Science Content Standards for California Public Schools. http://www.cde.ca.gov.

14. This activity was originally brought to teachers by Pilar Gray-Luzzi. It is cited in Education World's Millennium Series (1996–2003). *Five times five: Five activities for teaching geography's five themes.* http://www.education-world.com/a_lesson/lesson071.html. It incorporates the Colorado Model Content Standards for Geography. http://www.cde.state.co.us/cdeassess/geog.html.

15. California Department of Education. (1998, October). Social Science Content Standards for California Public Schools. http://www.cde.ca.gov.

CHAPTER TWO

1. Vygotsky, L. S. (1978). *Mind in society: The development of higher psychological processes* (M. Cole, V. John-Steiner, S. Scribner, & E. Souberman, Eds. and Trans.). Cambridge, MA: Harvard University Press.

2. Dalton, S. S. (1998). *Pedagogy matters: Standards for effective teaching practice.* Santa Cruz, CA: Center for Research on Education, Diversity and Excellence.

3. These focus questions were developed: (a) in collaboration in the summer of 2003 with Lucia Villareal, a nationally–board certified master teacher at Starlight Elementary School, and (b) from Stephanie Dalton's work: Dalton, S. (1998). *Pedagogy matters: Standards for effective teaching practice.* Santa Cruz, CA: Center for Research on Education, Diversity and Excellence.

4. Parker, R .C. (2003). *Teaching diverse learners.* Providence, RI: Education Alliance at Brown University. P. 2. http://www.lab.brown.edu/tdl/tl-strategies/mc-principles-prt.shtml.

5. Walqui, A. (2000, June). *Strategies for success: Engaging immigrant students in secondary schools.* San Francisco: ERIC Clearinghouse on Languages and Linguistics. http://www.cal.org/ericcll/digest/0003strategies.html.

6. California Department of Education. (1997, December). Mathematics Content Standards for California Public Schools. http://www.cde.ca.gov/board/pdf/mathematics.pdf.

7. California Department of Education. (1998, October). California State Board of Education Earth Sciences Standards. http://www.cde.ca.gov/be/st/ss/scearth.asp.

8. This lesson was originally created and taught by Susan Freeman in fall 1998 and is used with permission.

9. Walqui. (2000, June).

10. California Department of Education. (1999, July). English-Language Development Standards for California Public Schools. http://www.cde.ca.gov/re/pn/fd/documents/englangdev-stnd.pdf.

11. California Department of Education. (1998, October). Science Content Standards for California Public Schools. http://www.cde.ca.gov/board/pdf/science.pdf.

12. Porritt, J. (1994). *Save the earth.* Newbury Park, CA: Haynes Publications.

13. *Literacy and learning: Reading in the content areas.* (1999). http://www.litandlearn.lpb.org/strategies/strat_quick.pdf.

14. Wiggins, G., & McTighe, J. (1998). *Understanding by design.* Alexandria, VA: Association for Supervision and Curriculum Development. Many teachers have studied and applied the *Understanding by Design* model to their teaching. Part of lesson and unit planning involves determining "key design questions," which require teachers to ponder, "What types of questions might guide our teaching and engage students in uncovering the important ideas at the heart of each subject?"

15. Cited in Porritt (1994).

CHAPTER THREE

1. Lee, E. (1994). Taking multicultural, anti-racist education seriously: An interview with Enid Lee. In B. Bigelow, L. Christensen, S. Karp, B. Miner, & B. Peterson (Eds.), *Rethinking our classrooms: Teaching for equity and justice* (PP. 19–22). Milwaukee, WI: Rethinking Schools Limited. P. 20.

2. For more information on service-learning, go to http://www.learningindeed.org and http://www.kidsforcommunity.org. Also see: Eyler, J., & Giles, D. E. Jr. (1999). *Where's the learning in service-learning?* San Francisco: Jossey-Bass. Stanton, T. K., Giles, D. E. Jr., & Cruz, N. I. (1999). *Service-learning: A movement's pioneers reflect on its origins, practice, and future.* San Francisco: Jossey-Bass.

3. National Council of Teachers of Mathematics. (2005). NCTM standards. Reston, VA: National Council of Teachers of Mathematics. http://standards.nctm.org. National Research Council of the National Science Teachers Association. (1995). *National science education standards.* Arlington, VA: National Research Council of the National Science Teachers Association. http://www.nsta.org/standards.

4. International Reading Association and National Council of Teachers of English. (1996). *Standards for the English language arts.* Newark, DE: International Reading Association and National Council of Teachers of English. http://www.reading.org/resources/issues/reports/learning_standards.html.

5. August, D., & Hakuta, K. (1998). *Educating language minority children.* Washington, DC: National Academy Press, 31–38.

6. Tharp, R., & Entz, S. (2003, September). From high chair to high school: Research-based principles for teaching complex thinking. *Young Children, 58*(5), 38–43.

7. Poplin, M., & Weeres, J. (1994). *Voices from the inside: A report on schooling from inside the classroom.* Claremont, CA: Institute for Education in Transformation at the Claremont Graduate School.

8. These focus questions were developed: (a) in collaboration in the summer of 2003 with Lucia Villareal, a nationally–board certified master teacher at Starlight Elementary School, and (b) from Stephanie Dalton's work: Dalton, S. (1998). *Pedagogy matters: Standards for effective teaching practice.* Santa Cruz, CA: Center for Research on Education, Diversity and Excellence.

9. This lesson was created by Diane Ichikawa, who thanks the Japanese American Citizens League. She was inspired to teach this lesson by referencing the league's curriculum guides. For educational purposes, I have made adaptations to its original form. Although I use Diane's name to honor her contribution, the lesson and the commentary have been adapted from several other teachers' experiences.

10. Houston, J., & Houston, J. D. (1973). *Farewell to Manzanar: A true story of Japanese American experience during and after the World War II internment.* New York: Random House. Frank, A. (1993). *Anne Frank: The diary of a young girl.* New York: Bantam. Uchida, Y. (1984). *Desert exile: The uprooting of a Japanese American family.* Seattle: University of Washington Press.

11. California Department of Education. (1997, December). Language Arts Content Standards for California Public Schools. http://www.cde.ca.gov/board/pdf/reading.pdf.

12. California Department of Education. (1998, October). Science Content Standards for California Public Schools. http://www.cde.ca.gov/board/pdf/science.pdf.

13. Menzel, P. (1995). *Material World: A Global Family Portrait.* San Francisco: Sierra Club Books.

14. California Department of Education. (1998, October). Social Science Content Standards for California Public Schools. http://www.cde.ca.gov/board/pdf/reading.pdf.

15. August and Hakuta. (1998).

16. Chávez Chávez, R. (1997). *A curriculum discourse for achieving equity: Implications for teachers when engaged with Latina and Latino students.* Las Cruces: New Mexico State University.

CHAPTER FOUR

1. Tharp, R. G. (1997). *From at-risk to excellence: Research, theory, and principles for practice.* Santa Cruz: University of California, Santa Cruz: Center for Research on Education, Diversity and Excellence. P. 8.

2. Tharp. (1997, p. 8).

3. These focus questions were developed: (a) in collaboration in the summer of 2003 with Lucia Villareal, a nationally–board certified master teacher at Starlight Elementary School, and (b) from Stephanie Dalton's work: Dalton, S. (1998). *Pedagogy matters: Standards for effective teaching practice.* Santa Cruz, CA: Center for Research on Education, Diversity and Excellence.

4. Tharp. (1997, P. 8).

5. These cooperative learning strategies belong to the work of Kagan, S. (1994). *Cooperative learning.* San Clements, CA: Kagan Cooperative Learning.

6. Angelou, M. (1983). *I know why the caged bird sings.* New York: Bantam.

7. For great ideas on writing rubrics, I referred to the following Web sites to build the Maya Angelou editorial writing assignment rubric:

   http://www.rubrics4teachers.com/ and http://school.discovery.com/schrockguide.assess.html#rubrics.

8. California Department of Education. (1997, December). English-Language Arts Content Standards for California Public Schools. http://www.cde.ca.gov/re/pn/fd/documents/english-language-arts.pdf.

9. California Department of Education. (1998, October). History–Social Science Content Standards for California Public Schools. http://www.cde.ca.gov/board/pdf/history.pdf.

10. California Department of Education. (1997, December). *Mathematics Content Standards for California Public Schools.* http://www.cde.ca.gov/ci/ma/cf/.

11. The Math Forum. http://mathforum.org/library/drmath/drmath.high.html.

12. The National Language Arts Standards (International Reading Association and National Council of Teachers of English, 1996) and the Social Sciences Standards (National Council for the Social Studies, 1994) are posted at http://www.education-world.com/standards/.

13. The research rubric was developed from several sources, including http://www.teachervision.fen.com/lesson-plans/lesson-2171.html.

14. Alvarez, A. (1995). *In the time of butterflies.* New York: Plume Publishers.

15. Tharp, R. G., Estrada, P., Dalton, S. S., & Yamauchi, L. (2000). *Teaching transformed: Achieving excellence, fairness, inclusion, and harmony.* Boulder, CO: Westview Press. P. 30.

CHAPTER FIVE

1. Tharp, R. G., & Gallimore, R. (1988). *Rousing minds to life: Teaching, learning, and schooling in social context.* Cambridge: Cambridge University Press.

2. Goldenberg, C. (1992). *Instructional conversations and their classroom application.* Santa Cruz, CA: University of California, National Center for Research on Cultural Diversity and Second Language Learning. (ERIC Document Reproduction Service No. EDO-FL-92–01) Description and development of the instructional conversation has taken place over the past thirty years. The original concept and defined teaching practice is documented in Tharp & Gallimore. (1988). It has been further developed by a number of educational researchers, including S. S. Dalton, C. Goldenberg, R. Rueda, L. A. Yamauchi, J. Echevarria, J. C. Jordan, K. Au, & R. McDonough.

3. Sirota, A. J. (1997). *The development of knowledge and understandings in four preservice teachers: A sociocultural perspective.* Unpublished master's thesis, University of California.

4. These focus questions were developed: (a) in collaboration in the summer of 2003 with Lucia Villareal, a nationally–board certified master teacher at Starlight Elementary School, and (b) from Stephanie Dalton's work: Dalton, S. (1998). *Pedagogy matters: Standards for effective teaching practice.* Santa Cruz, CA: Center for Research on Education, Diversity and Excellence.

5. Tharp, R. G., Rivera, H., Youpa, D. G., Dalton, S. S., Guardino, G. M., & Lasky, S. (1998). *Activity setting observation system (ASOS) coding rulebook.* Santa Cruz: University of California, Santa Cruz, Center for Research on Education, Diversity and Excellence.

6. The research is documented in Tharp, R. G., Estrada, P., Dalton, S. S., & Yamauchi, L. (2000). *Teaching transformed: Achieving excellence, fairness, inclusion, and harmony.* Boulder, CO: Westview Press.

7. This section is taken from Brigham Young University/Center for Research on Education, Diversity and Excellence. (2001). *Matrix Template for Interactive CDROM Case Studies: Inclusive Pedagogy/CREDE Content Area Classroom Series.* Unpublished manuscript, University of California, Santa Cruz.

8. McGinty, I. (1998). *Literature studies circles: Possible steps for implementation.* Unpublished manuscript. These cue cards were created in partnership with students and teachers at Starlight Elementary School and Hall District.

9. This lesson plan was developed from the work of Mara Mills, a former science teacher at Santa Cruz High School, and Joy Brewster, curriculum writer, editor, and consultant. Retrieved from http://school.discovery.com/lessonplans/programs/iceman/.

10. National Research Council. (1996). *National Science Education Standards.* http://www.nap.edu/readingroom/bools/nses/html.

11. National Council for the Social Studies. (1994). *National Social Science Standards.* www.education-world.com/standards/national/soc_sci/index.shtml.

12. Hayes, S. (December 8, 1997). What is a war crime? *Scholastic Update,* 12–14.

CONCLUSION

1. The Greenlandic Education Delegation is working in consultation with the Center for Research on Education, Diversity and Excellence to integrate the principles into their new educational reform program.

2. Native Americans use seven principles because they believe the last two, modeling/demonstration and student choice, are critical and culturally compatible with their school system. For more information, see Tharp, R. G., Lewis, H., Hilberg, R., Bird, C., Epaloose, G., Dalton, S. S., Youpa, D. G., Rivera, H., Riding In-Feathers, M., & Eriacho, W. (1999). Seven more mountains and a map: Overcoming obstacles to reform in Native American schools. *Journal of Education for Students Placed at Risk, 4*(1), 5–26.

3. Tharp, R. G., & Gallimore, R. (1988). *Rousing minds to life: Teaching, learning, and schooling in social context.* Cambridge: Cambridge University Press.

APPENDIX 1

1. Center for Research on Education, Diversity and Excellence. (2002). *Research evidence: Five standards for effective pedagogy and student outcomes.* Santa Cruz: University of California, Santa Cruz, Center for Research on Education, Diversity and Excellence.

2. Kagan, S. (1994). *Cooperative learning.* San Clements, CA: Kagan Cooperative Learning.

3. Kagan. (1994).

Index

A

Adolescents, working with, 11–12

Assessment: biology lesson (joint productive activity), 18; Castle Building, Middle Ages Unit (joint productive activity), 27; Create an Island lesson (joint productive activity), 18; Examining the Environment (language development revised lesson), 47; Exploring Culture Activity (contextualization), 68; Geometry Construction (language development lesson), 34–35; of instructional conversation, 105; of joint productive activities, 13; of learning centers, 131–132; mathematics lesson (language development), 34–35; rubric for the castle activity, 28; social science lesson (instructional conversation), 119; social science lesson (language development), 47; War and Conflict Instructional Conversation (teaching through dialogue lesson), 119; world history/geography lesson (contextualization), 68; world history lesson (joint productive activity), 27

B

Back-to-basics curriculum, 4–5

Biology lesson (contextualization), 61–65; collage project, 61–65; collage project instructions (handout), 62; collage project rubric, 63; commentary, 64; ecology science standards, 61; learning objectives, 64; lesson plan, 62

Biology lesson (instructional conversation), 105–113; commentary, 112–113; conduct of lesson, 108–112; connection question, 108–109; Forensic Science (lesson), 106–120; homework/seatwork, 112; joint venture, 112; learning objectives, 107; lesson plan, 107–108; National Science standards, 106; text support, 110–111; weaving question, 109

Biology lesson (joint productive activity), 17–18; biology standard and learning goal, 19; commentary, 22; conduct of lesson, 18–21; Create an Island reflection questions, 21; Create an Island student instructions (handout), 19–20; instructions, 19–20; learning objectives, 17; lesson assessment, 18; lesson plan, 17–18; standard in biology, 17

Brainstorm web, 37

C

Castle building, Middle Ages Unit (joint productive activity), 22–28; assessment rubric for the castle activity, 28; castle-building activity (handout), 25; castle questions (handout), 24; commentary, 27; conduct of lesson, 23; learning objectives, 23; lesson assessment, 27; lesson plan, 23; world history standards, 23

Challenging activities, 75–96

Classroom conversation schedule (example), 103

Closed (dead-end) questions, 91

Collage project (contextualization), 61–65; commentary, 64; instructions (handout), 62; learning objectives, 64; lesson plan, 64; rubric, 63

Community outreach, and context for learning, 57

Complex thinking, teaching, 75–96; focus questions for planning lessons, 76; lessons from the classroom, 76–95; literature lesson, 77–84; mathematics lesson, 87–89; social science lesson, 84–87, 90–95

Complex World of Teaching, The (Mintz and Yun), 53, 75

Conceptual foundation, 89

Content goals, and instructional conversation, 100

Contextualizing instruction, 53–74; biology lesson, 61–65; within the community, 54–56; cultural compatibility, 55; focus questions for planning lessons, 57; history/social studies lesson, 70–71; language arts/history lesson, 58–61; lessons/activities, 56–57; lessons from the classroom, 57–73; research support, 55–56; world history/geography lesson, 65–70

Cooperative learning, 10–11, 29

Create an Island lesson (joint productive activity), 17–18; biology standard and learning goal, 19; commentary, 22; conduct of lesson, 18–21; instructions, 19–20; learning objectives, 17; lesson assessment, 18; lesson plan, 17–18; reflection questions, 21; standard in biology, 17; student instructions (handout), 19–20

Culture wheel template, 67

D

De-automatization, 98

Demographics, changes in, 2

Desert Exile (Uchida), 58

Diary of Anne Frank, The, 58–60

Diversification of activities, in public education, 6

E

Earth sciences lesson (language development), 36–40; commentary, 40; conduct of lesson, 40; learning objectives, 37; lesson plan, 37; plate tectonics language activity, 36–40; Plate Tectonics Word Web Activity (handout), 38; science and technology standards, 36–37; word web, 37; What's a Word Web? (handout), 39

Economics, and public education, 3

English Language Learners: challenging activities for, 75–84; and instructional conversation, 99, 102; and quality educational programs, 76

Examining the Environment (language development lesson), 45–51; commentary, 45–46; lesson plan, 45; standards, 45

Examining the Environment (language development revised lesson), 46–51; commentary, 47; learning objectives, 46; lesson assessment, 47; lesson plan, 46–47; Quick-Write Activity (handout), 48; Research Tasks for PowerPoint Presentation (handout), 49; rubric for grading literary responses: environment unit, 50–51; standards, 46

Exploring Culture Activity (contextualization), 66–70; commentary, 68; culture wheel template, 67; essential lesson goals, 66; lesson assessment, 67; lesson plan, 66, 68; social science standards, 66; student's culture wheel, 67; universal culture wheel, 69

Extensions, providing, 89

F

Families of the Coastside (handout), 71

Farewell to Manzanar (Houston/Houston), 57–60

Focus questions: defined, 12; instructional conversation, 99–100; joint productive activities, 13; language development, 32

Focus questions for planning lessons: complex thinking, teaching, 76; contextualizing instruction, 57

Forensic Science (teaching through dialogue lesson), 106–120; commentary, 112–113; conduct of lesson, 108–110; connection question,

108–109; homework/seatwork, 112; joint product, 112; learning objectives, 107; lesson plan, 107–108; National Science standards, 106; text support, 110–111; weaving question, 109

Foundations of Literacy, The (Holdaway), 31

G

Gatekeepers, teachers as, 52

Geometry construction (language development lesson), 33–36; learning objectives, 34; lesson assessment, 34–35; lesson conduct, 34–35; lesson plan, 34; mathematics standard, 34; revised lesson, 35–36; rubric for tent construction activity, 35

Global Studies lesson (instructional conversation), 113–120; commentary, 119–120; conduct of lesson, 115–119; connection question, 117; global issues lesson design, 114; homework/seatwork, 119; joint product, 119; learning objectives, 115; lesson assessment, 119; lesson plan, 115; samples of student work on the war and conflict unit, 121; Student Assignment for the Global Reading Center Human Rights Task: What Is a War Crime? (handout), 116; text support, 118–119; War and Conflict Instructional Conversation (lesson), 115–120; weaving question, 117–118

Global Studies lesson (language development), 44–51; commentary, 45–46, 47; Examining the Environment, 45–51; learning objectives, 46; lesson assessment, 47; lesson plan, 45, 46–47; Quick-Write Activity (handout), 48; Research Tasks for PowerPoint Presentation (handout), 49; rubric for grading literary responses: environment unit, 50–51; standards, 45, 46

Global Warming Activity (lesson), 85–87; commentary, 87; conduct of lesson, 85; learning objectives, 85; lesson plan, 85; social science standards, 85; Student Assignment for "Our Environment: Global Warming" (handout), 86

Greenlandic Education Delegation, 123

Greenlandic mythology, 123

H

High School Leadership Summit (U.S. Secretary of Education), 10

History/social studies lesson (contextualization), 69–70; commentary, 70, 73; essential lesson goals, 69; Families of the Coastside (handout), 71; lesson plan, 70

Homeless Garden Project, 65

I

I Know Why the Caged Bird Sings (lesson), 79; commentary, 79; lesson plan, 79; Maya Angelou literary analysis rubric, 80

I Know Why the Caged Bird Sings (revised lesson), 83; commentary, 83–84; essential standards, 83; learning objectives, 83; lesson plan, 83; Maya Angelou editorial writing assignment rubric, 82; Student Assignment for *I Know Why the Caged Bird Sings* Lesson (handout), 81

In the Time of Butterflies (Alvarez), 95

Instructional conversation, 97–121; assessing, 105; benefits of, 99; biology lesson, 105–113; classroom conversation schedule (example), 103; connection questions, 101; content areas for, 98; conversational activities, organizing, 100–105; defined, 97; differentiated instruction, 104; focus questions, 99–100; follow-up seatwork/homework, 101; joint production/conclusion, 101; learning to incorporate into teaching, 120; lessons from the classroom, 105–121; participation structure cards, 103–104; planning lessons with, 99–100; power of, 98; sequence, 101; social science lesson, 113–120; structuring, 100; student participation, encouraging, 102; teacher's role, 98; text support, 101; time management, 102; weaving questions, 101

J

Joint productive activities: assessment of, 13; biology lesson, 17–18; creating lessons with, 12–13; defined, 9; focus questions, 13; implementation of strategy, 10; and learning centers, 127; and learning diversification, 9; lessons from the classroom, 15–27; literature lesson, 15–17; research support for, 10–11; structuring, elements necessary for, 12–13; teacher's role, 12; world history lesson, 22–28

L

Lack of relevance, 3

Language arts/history lesson (contextualization): commentary, 60–61; examples of student quick-writes, 59; learning objectives, 58; lesson plan for literary analysis, 60; lesson plan for role play, 58–59; standards: literary response and analysis for grades 6 to 9, 58; Tragedies of War: The Japanese Internment (lesson), 58

Language development, 31–52; earth sciences lesson, 36–40; enacting the principle of, 31; focus questions, 32; lessons from the classroom, 33–51; mathematics lesson, 33–36; scaffolding, defined, 32; scaffolding instruction, 32; Sheltered English lesson, 40–44; social sciences lesson, 44–51

Language goals, and instructional conversation, 100

Learning centers, 10, 127–132; assessment, 131–132; center activities, 127–128; classroom groupings, 129; defined, 127; group management and discipline, 129–130; learning center and lecture schedule, 130; organizing, 128–129; rights and responsibilities (table), 130; scheduling activities, 130–132; self-contained, 128–129

Literature lesson (complex thinking), 77–84; commentary, 79, 83–84; essential standards, 83; learning objectives, 83; lesson plan, 79, 83; Maya Angelou editorial writing assignment rubric, 82; Maya Angelou literary analysis rubric, 80; reflection questions, 77; Student Assignment for *I Know Why the Caged Bird Sings* (handout), 81; *I Know Why the Caged Bird Sings* (lesson), 79; *I Know Why the Caged Bird Sings* (revised lesson), 83

Literature lesson (joint productive activity), 15–17; commentary, 16–17; conduct of lesson, 16; learning objectives, 15; lesson plan, 16; standards for literary response and analysis, 15; Time, Sequence, and Setting in Literature (lesson), 15–17

M

Making meaning, *See* Contextualizing instruction
Material World: A Global Family Portrait (Menzel), 65

Math Forum Web site, 89

Mathematics lesson (complex thinking), 87–89; commentary, 88–89; essential mathematics standards, 88; lesson plan, 88; Trigonometry (lesson), 86–89

Mathematics lesson (language development), 33–36; learning objectives, 34; lesson assessment, 34–35; lesson conduct, 34–35; lesson plan, 34; mathematics standard, 34; revised lesson, 35–36; rubric for tent construction activity, 35

Mind map, 37

N

Nation at Risk report, 4

National Science Education Standards, 106

National Science Standards, 55

No Child Left Behind Act, 4

O

Office of Vocational and Adult Education, U.S. Department of Education, 10

Open-ended questions, 91, 94

P

Pair share, 9–10, 22; defined, 9; involving students in, 89

Paradigm of public education, 2–3

Participation structure cards, 103–104

Plate Tectonics Language Activity (language development lesson), 36–40; commentary, 40; conduct of lesson, 40; learning objectives, 37;

lesson plan, 37; plate tectonics language activity, 36–40; Plate Tectonics Word Web Activity (handout), 38; science and technology standards, 36–37; word web, 37; What's a Word Web? (handout), 39

Power of Their Ideas, The (Meier), 1

Properties of Food, The (handout), 42

Public education: back-to-basics curriculum, 4–5; background theory, 6–7; changing demographics, 2; curriculum, 3–4; diversification of activities, 6; and economics, 3; five pedagogy principles for teaching and learning, 7; lack of relevance, 3; modifying teaching, 5; paradigm of, 2–3; solutions to problems of, 4–7; teaching force, 2; whole language movement, 4–5

Q

Quick-Write Activity (handout), 48

Quick write, defined, 45

R

Reading comprehension, and instructional conversation, 99

Recursion, 98

Relevance, lack of, 3

Research support, for joint productive activities, 10–11

Rights/responsibilities, learning centers, 130

Rousing Minds to Life (Tharp and Gallimore), 123

S

Save the Earth (Porritt), 45, 47–48

Scaffolding, 102; defined, 32

Scaffolding instruction, 32

Self-talk, 98

Semantic web, 37

Service-learning, 53–54

Sheltered English, defined, 40–41

Sheltered English lesson (language development), 40–44; commentary, 44; conduct of lesson, 43–44; expository reading activity, 41–44; learning objectives, 41; lesson plan, 41;

Properties of Food, The (handout), 42; sample of student work for expository reading, 43; standards for English language development, 41

Small-group conversational etiquette, and instructional conversation, 102

Social science lesson (complex thinking), 84–87, 90–95; commentary, 87, 92, 94; conduct of lesson, 85; Global Warming Activity (lesson), 85–87; learning objectives, 90; lesson plan, 85, 91–92; lesson plan, for generating research paragraphs, 92; lesson plan, for research (one to three periods), 92; lesson plan, for writing appropriate research questions (one to two periods), 91; research paper rubric, 93; social science standards, 85; standard (literature and social science), 90; Student Assignment for "Our Environment: Global Warming" (handout), 86; Writing Research Papers (lesson), 90–95

Student's culture wheel, 67

T

Taschek, Laura Ianacone, 13–14, 22–28, 45–51, 57, 65, 84–87, 90–95, 104, 113–120, 127–128

Teachers, as gatekeepers, 52

Teaching through dialogue, transformative potential of, 97; *See also* Instructional conversation

Tent construction activity, rubric for, 35

Think pair share, 9–10; defined, 9

Time, Sequence, and Setting in Literature (literature lesson), 15–17; commentary, 16–17; conduct of lesson, 16; learning objectives, 15; lesson plan, 16; standards for literary response and analysis, 15

Tragedies of War: The Japanese Internment (contextualization), 58–61; commentary, 60–61; examples of student quick-writes, 59; learning objectives, 58; lesson plan for literary analysis, 60; lesson plan for role play, 58–59; standards: literary response and analysis for grades 6 to 9, 58

Trigonometry (lesson), 86–89; commentary, 88–89; lesson plan, 88

U

Universal culture wheel, 69

V

Voices from the Inside, 56

W

War and Conflict Instructional Conversation (teaching through dialogue lesson), 115–120; commentary, 119–120; conduct of lesson, 115; connection question, 117; homework/seatwork, 119; joint product, 119; learning objectives, 115; lesson assessment, 119; lesson plan, 115; samples of student work on, 121; Student Assignment for the Global Reading Center Human Rights Task: What Is a War Crime?, 116; text support, 118–119; weaving question, 117–118

What's a Word Web? (handout), 39

Whole language movement, 4–5

Word web, 37

World history/geography lesson (contextualization), 65–70; commentary, 68; culture wheel template, 67; essential lesson goals, 66; Exploring Culture Activity (lesson), 66–70; lesson assessment, 68; lesson plan, 66, 70; social science standards, 66; student's culture wheel, 67; universal culture wheel, 69

World history lesson (joint productive activity), 22–28; assessment rubric for the castle activity, 28; castle-building activity (handout), 25–27; castle questions (handout), 24; commentary, 27; conduct of lesson, 23; learning objectives, 23; lesson assessment, 27; lesson plan, 23; world history standards, 23

Writing Research Papers (lesson), 90–95; commentary, 92, 94; learning objectives, 90; lesson plan for generating research paragraphs, 92; lesson plan for research (one to three periods), 92; lesson plan for writing appropriate research questions (one to two periods), 91; research paper rubric, 93; standard (literature and social science), 90

Z

Zone of proximal development (ZPD), 98